POCKET

KRAKÓW

TOP SIGHTS • LOCAL EXPERIENCES

MARK BAKER

Contents

Plan Your Trip   4

Town Hall Tower (p41)
RAGA / GETTY IMAGES ©

Welcome to Kraków

If you believe the legends, Kraków was founded on the defeat of a dragon, and it's true that a mythical atmosphere permeates its medieval streets and squares. However, there's more to this royal, regal former Polish capital than history and myth. The squares and alleyways pulse with modern life – creating a harmonious, infectious blend of past and present.

Top Sights

TANYASAV / GETTY IMAGES ©

Wawel Royal Castle

Potent symbol of Polish identity. **p36**

ENDLESS TRAVEL / ALAMY STOCK PHOTO ©

Rynek Underground

Modern wizardry meets Middle Ages. **p54**

St Mary's Basilica

Kraków's signature Gothic church. **p52**

Collegium Maius

A primer in medieval science. **p56**

Schindler's Factory

Interactive account of German occupation. **p102**

Galicia Jewish Museum

Jewish history reimagined in photos. **p78**

Wieliczka Salt Mine

Underground splendours crafted from salt. **p140**

BEAUTIFUL LANDSCAPE / SHUTTERSTOCK ©

PRASZKIEWICZ / SHUTTERSTOCK ©

Auschwitz-Birkenau Memorial & Museum

An essential, terrible history lesson. **p136**

Eating

Kraków is a food paradise. The Old Town is packed with venues catering for every pocket. Many are housed in vaulted cellars or courtyards. Aside from Polish places, you'll find Italian, French, Indian, Middle Eastern, Japanese, Mexican and more. Many restaurants in Kazimierz offer Jewish-themed cooking.

Polish Cooking

You can't say you've eaten Polish food until you've had many plates of *pierogi*, the crescent-shaped dumplings that are stuffed with cheese, minced meat or sauerkraut. You might want to try *gołąbki* (cabbage leaves stuffed with beef and rice), but don't confuse them with *golonka* (boiled pig's knuckle). Everywhere you'll find food that's both filling and delicious.

Dining on a Budget

There is no shortage of fine-dining establishments, but budget travellers will also be delighted by their options. Kraków has plenty of low-cost eateries called *bar mleczny* (milk bars). They offer affordable and filling Polish food, often served cafeteria-style so you know exactly what you're getting. Other options include the many student-oriented vegetarian and vegan food bars around town.

Street Food

Kraków has loads of street-food options to keep you nourished between meals. *Obwarzanek* are hefty pretzels sold from street vendors around town. Kazimierz, specifically Plac Nowy, is ground zero for 'Polish pizza' – *zapiekanka* (pictured). It's half a baguette, topped with cheese, ham and mushrooms. The food-truck scene is here too. Find a clutch of mobile food-sellers a couple of blocks southeast of Plac Nowy.

JACKF / GETTY IMAGES ©

Best Polish Food

U Babci Maliny Excellent value, traditional Polish. (p68)

Sąsiedzi High-tone mains like goose and duck show a different side to Polish cooking. (p90)

Miód Malina Wawel favourite specialises in countrified cooking. (p46)

Pod Aniołami You'll find wild boar on the menu to match the Gothic cellar setting. (p46)

Best Vegetarian & Vegan

Youmiko Sushi Vegan sushi to die for; Sundays are 'all-vegan'. (p90)

Glonojad Well-done salads, beans, pastas and pierogi. (p121)

Restauracja Pod Norenami Asian-inspired noodles, dumplings and curries. (p121)

Veganic High-tone vegetarian in a shabby-chic drawing-room setting. (p121)

Best for Lunch

Krako Slow Wines Culinary oasis in the food desert around Schindler's Factory. (p109)

Chimera Salad Bar High-quality salad bar within easy walk of the Old Town sites. (p67)

Hawełka Good-value luncheon specials in an art nouveau setting. (p68)

Hummus Amamamusi Yummy, artisanal hummus flavoured any way you like. (p92)

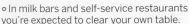

Dining Tips

○ In milk bars and self-service restaurants you're expected to clear your own table.

○ Expect slow service. To speed things up, grab your own menu when you enter a restaurant; they will likely be stacked by the door.

Drinking & Nightlife

The Main Market Square is ringed with bars and cafes whose outdoor tables offer great people-watching spots. Kazimierz also has a lively bar scene centred on Plac Nowy and surrounding streets. The area around Plac Wolnica in the western part of Kazimierz has blossomed in recent years into another cafe/bar cluster.

Bar or Cafe?

In Kraków, it's not often easy to tell the difference. The drinking scene is dominated by two types of venues: creative cafes that also serve alcohol; and bohemian bars that also serve coffee. In both, you can also normally grab a bite to eat. Indeed, whatever the primary purpose, Kraków specialises in places with an artsy atmosphere, usually furnished with mismatched chairs and tables, eclectic artwork and casually cool-looking patrons.

Not too posh, but not too pleb either.

Vodka & Beer

The Polish national drink, vodka (*wódka*), is normally drunk as a shot. Clear vodka is not the only species of the spirit. Indeed, there's a whole spectrum of varieties of vodka, from sweet to extra dry. Polish drinking habits are changing, though, with tastes turning to beer (*piwo*) instead of (or in addition to) vodka. You'll find several brands of good Polish *piwo*, such as

Żywiec, Tyskie, Okocim and Lech, as well as a growing number of craft breweries.

Best Cafes

BAL Trendy coffee joint in the neighbourhood behind Schindler's Factory. (p113)

Mleczarnia Sip by candlelight at this old-school Kazimierz coffeehouse. (p96)

Cafe Pianola The coffee is good but don't miss those Renaissance interiors. (p48)

Dziórawy Kocioł Kids will love the spooky Harry Potter tie-ins. (p48)

Meho Cafe The lovely garden is a piece of solitude on a busy street. (p125)

HEMIS / ALAMY STOCK PHOTO ©

Best Bars

Forum Przestrzenie
Combination of great drinks
and a choice riverside locale.
(p112)

Piwiarnia Warka Good
sports bar with a relaxing
terrace for people-watching.
(p123)

Pauza Hip Old Town
watering hole with an arty,
intellectual vibe. (p71)

Spokój This retro hideaway,
with a campy '70s decor,
feels like a find. (p70)

Cocktails & Craft Beers

Mercy Brown This secretive
place might be Kraków's
quirkiest bar. (p123)

Weźże Krafta Rarely a free
table at this Tytano-complex
shrine to craft beers. (p123)

T.E.A. Time Brew Pub Drop
by for a glass of real ale
brewed on site. (p97)

Zaraz Wracam Tu No frills
cocktail bar with a creative
take on 'doing shots'. (p132)

Lindo Gay-friendly cocktail
within easy walk of the Main
Market Square. (p70)

Best Clubs

Hevre This former Jewish
prayer house comes alive
weekend nights. (p95)

Scena54 Tytano-based
dance club caters to revelers
of all ages. (p123)

Feniks Red-velvet curtains
and white tablecloths lend a
classy vibe. (p71)

Klub Spolem Underground
club with lots of throwback
communist kitsch. (pic-
tured; p71)

Shopping

Kraków has a vast array of shops, selling everything from tacky T-shirts to exquisite crystal glassware. Most shops of interest are in the Old Town and Kazimierz. An obvious place to start your hunt is at the souvenir market within the Cloth Hall (p62) at the Main Market Square.

Polish Souvenirs

If you're in the market for the perfect Polish souvenir, you'll have plenty of choices in Kraków. You can't go wrong with typical food and drink. One staple is Polish vodka, but the country also turns out good chocolates, honey and jam. Poland is known for glassware and ceramics, particularly the colourful plates, jugs and vases from the western town of Bolesławiec.

Amber, Amber, Amber

Amber, otherwise known as 'Baltic gold', is fossilised tree resin, usually found on the shores of the Baltic Sea. When it's cut and buffed it makes for a beautiful semi-precious 'stone' (pictured) in a ring, necklace or brooch, and Kraków has plenty of galleries with beautiful and original designs and settings. Make sure to look around as prices can vary considerably.

Antiques & Flea Markets

Kraków is an excellent spot for antique and thrift shopping. The Old Town is home to many of the more upscale places, with beautifully refurbished antique jewellery, watches and accessories, while Kazimierz is good for sifting through discarded items that might charitably be called junk (but you never know when you might find that gem).

LERNER VADIM / SHUTTERSTOCK ©

Gifts & Souvenirs

Kacper Ryx Astounding collection of Polish gifts. (p74)

Asortyment Shop Souvenir baskets, ceramics and other small items made exclusively in Poland. (p99)

Kobalt Pottery & More Plates, cups and vases sporting eye-catching designs from the workshop at Bolesławiec. (p49)

Schubert World of Amber A celebration of all things made from that pretty petrified resin. (p49)

Best Polish Design

Szpeje Retro posters, postcards and coffee cups from communist days. (p83)

Galeria Plakatu Dusty old shop featuring classic movie posters. (p74)

Dydo Poster Gallery Striking poster art. (p125)

Paon Nonchalant Fashionable women's clothing and accessories from exclusively Polish designers. (p98)

Lookarna Illustrations Original hand-drawn postcards, posters, bookmarks. (p99)

Best Antique & Junk Shops

Rubin Carefully chosen selection of antique jewellery, silver pieces and old watches. (p75)

Salon Antyków Pasja Three rooms stuffed with old maps, furniture, paintings and clocks. (p75)

Antykwariat na Kazimierzu The shambolic basement of the **Judaica Foundation** is filled with bric-a-brac. (p99)

Market Treasures

For everything from rusty war relics to attractive collectables, check out the flea market on Sunday mornings at **Unitarg Hala Targowa** (ul Grzegórzecka 3; ⏱7am-3pm, to noon Sun; 🚋1, 17, 19, 22) in Eastern Kraków.

Historic Sites

The history of Poland's former royal capital reads like an epic novel, filled with plenty of periods when it seems all is lost, only to have greatness restored at the very last moment.

Royal Capital

Kraków became the capital of Poland in 1038 and was centred near Wawel Royal Castle. The capital was burned to the ground in 1241 by marauding Tatars, but enterprising residents moved the city to its current location around the market square and surrounded it with impenetrable walls. Under the leadership of Kazimierz III Wielki (1333–70), the city thrived.

Demolition & Decline

The city's status slipped in 1596 when Poland's capital was moved to a rival city, Warsaw, though Kraków remained the site of coronations and royal burials. The move prompted several centuries of decline, culminating in a decision by the occupying Austrian Empire to relegate the city to the peripheral province of Galicia in the 19th century.

World War & Communism

Following WWI, Kraków once again thrived – but another bout of tragedy was just around the corner with WWII. The German occupation led to the murder of the city's academic elite and the slaughter of tens of thousands of Jewish citizens in the Holocaust. The communist government added more misery by building a heavily polluting steelworks at Nowa Huta.

AGSAZ / SHUTTERSTOCK ©

Best Royal History

Wawel Royal Castle The centre of power for five centuries and enduring emblem of the Polish state. (p36)

Collegium Maius The oldest surviving university building in Poland and symbol of national influence. (p56)

Cloth Hall Focal point of the Main Market Square and once the centre of Kraków's medieval cloth trade. (pictured; p62)

Best Churches

St Mary's Basilica The church's uneven towers are a symbol of the city. (p52)

Wawel Cathedral Witness to countless coronations and the final resting place

of Polish monarchs and heroes. (p38)

Basilica of St Francis Gorgeous church enlivened by Art Nouveau stained-glass windows. (p43)

Best Museums

Rynek Underground This 'Middle Ages meets 21st century' experience is

enhanced by holograms and audiovisual wizardry. (p54)

Museum of Pharmacy One of the best of its kind, with heaps of old lab equipment and rare pharmaceutical instruments. (p62)

Historical Museum of Kraków Iinteractive exhibition that charts the city from its earliest days to WWI. (p63)

Worth a Trip

Twelve kilometres southwest of the centre, the **Benedictine Abbey of SS Peter & Paul** (Opactwo Benedyktynów w Tyńcu; ☏12 688 5452; www.benedyktyni.eu; ul Benedyktyńska 37, Tyniec; admission free; ☉museum 10am-6pm; ☒112) rises on a cliff above the Vistula. To reach the abbey, take bus 112 or hop a bike and follow the path along the Vistula River.

Architecture

Poland's architecture styles have followed Western Europe over the centuries. The earliest style, Romanesque, dates from the 12th century, but little has survived. There are ample remnants, however, of Gothic, Renaissance, Baroque and Art Nouveau.

High Gothic

Gothic architecture, with its pointed arches and ribbed vaults, began in the 14th century and lasted around 200 years. It's associated with the prosperous reign of King Kazimierz III Wielki and is seen in important churches such as Wawel Cathedral and St Mary's Basilica.

Renaissance

Renaissance architecture originated in Italy and swept over Central Europe in the 1500s. Renaissance style coincided with the apex of Kraków's power. The best examples include the Cloth Hall on the Main Market Square and the courtyards at Wawel Royal Castle.

Baroque & Neoclassical

Baroque, strongly associated with the Catholic Church, swept aside almost all other styles by the 17th century. Lavish and highly decorative, it altered existing architecture by adding its sumptuous decor to interiors, particularly churches.

Art Nouveau & Socialist-Realist

The sinuous lines of Art Nouveau are evident in buildings embellished by local artists Józef Mehoffer and Stanisław Wyspiański. The lows came a few decades later in the communist period, though the Nowa Huta district shows off a more positive side of Socialist-Realist architecture.

Best Gothic

St Catherine's Church
Enormous 14th-century church has retained its original Gothic proportions. (p81)

VILLOREJO / SHUTTERSTOCK ©

City Defence Walls The Florian Gate was once the city's main entrance and dates from the 14th century. (p63)

Holy Trinity Basilica The Dominican Church is defined by its gorgeous Gothic portal. (p62)

Best Renaissance

Cloth Hall Exudes harmony and proportion from the centre of the Main Market Square. (p62)

Wawel Royal Castle The arcaded courtyards show off Kraków at the height of its power. (p36)

Best Baroque

Church of SS Peter & Paul Eye catching statues line the exterior of the city's first Baroque building. (p43)

Church of St Anne Considered one of Poland's best examples of classical Baroque. (p64)

Best Art Nouveau

Noworolski Peek inside this cafe to admire the stunning Art Nouveau interiors by Polish artist Józef Mehoffer. (pictured; p55)

Palace of Fine Arts The most impressive edifice on Art Nouveau–friendly Plac Szczepański. (p63)

Best Communist

Forum Przestrzenie The brutalist 1970s Hotel Forum has been given a retro makeover. (p112)

Arka Pana This modern church was the first place of worship built in Nowa Huta. (p135)

Teatr Ludowy Excellent example of stark Socialist-Realist architecture from the 1950s. (p135)

Architecture-Spotting

One of the few surviving remnants of Romanesque in Kraków can be seen in the facade of the **Church of St Andrew**. (p44)

Music

Southern Poland's leading cultural centre is no slouch when it comes to the performing arts, classical music and opera. Kraków has a long tradition in jazz and some of the country's most historic jazz clubs. Thousands of students ensure a lively club and indie scene, with some shows held in rehabbed factories and industrial sites.

JON AKIRA YAMAMOTO / CONTRIBUTOR / GETTY IMAGES ©

High-Brow Music Taste

Cracovians enjoy some world-class cultural institutions, including a strikingly modern opera house in the eastern part of the city and a philharmonic orchestra, which plays in its own space in the western part of town. The annual concert season runs from autumn to spring, and regular festivals and musical events pick up the slack in down times. The InfoKraków Old Town (p151) office can help get tickets.

Best Classical & Opera

Opera Krakowska The Kraków Opera performs in the striking, modern building, but the repertoire spans the ages. (p133)

Kraków Philharmonic Home to one of the best orchestras in the country. (pictured; p124)

Best for Jazz

Harris Piano Jazz Bar Serious jazz in an atmospheric cellar space below the Main Market Square. (p72)

Piano Rouge Opulent cellar club and restaurant. Music starts nightly at 9pm. (p74)

Jazz Club U Muniaka Well-known jazz outlet just a couple steps from the Main Market Square. (p73)

Best Live Music

Alchemia Landmark Kazimierz drinking spot holds gigs through the week. (p96)

Piwnica Pod Baranami Awesome pub, transformed some nights into cabaret, jazz bar or jam session. (p72)

Church Concerts

The **Church of SS Peter & Paul** regularly hosts evening concerts for tourists. Buy tickets at the door or at InfoKraków tourist information offices. (p49)

Art

As the former capital of a strongly Catholic country, Kraków has an amazing collection of religious art in churches and museums going back centuries. It was also centre of the Młoda Polska (Young Poland) movement in visual arts in the early 20th century that left the city with an impressive heritage of Art Nouveau works.

DEA PICTURE LIBRARY /
CONTRIBUTOR / GETTY IMAGES ©

'Lady With An Ermine'

Kraków's most valuable work of art is Leonardo da Vinci's masterpiece *Lady with an Ermine* (pictured). The 15th-century painting is one of just a handful of portraits Leonardo made of women. The Germans stole the painting in WWII and it was later returned by the Americans. Find it at the refurbished Czartoryski Museum (p62).

Best Museums

National Museum A treasure chest of early-modern weirdness from the likes of Stanisław Wyspiański. (p118)

Bishop Erazm Ciołek Palace Well-curated collection of religious and paintings dating from the 12th to 18th centuries. (p44)

Gallery of 19th-Century Polish Painting The Chełmoński room holds important works of the Realist, Impressionist and Symbolist schools. (p62)

Museum of Contemporary Art in Kraków Cutting-edge modern painting and visual arts, just beside Schindler's Factory. (p108)

Best Galleries

Raven Gallery Private gallery, lovingly curated, with numerous beautiful examples of modern paintings. (p83)

Starmach Gallery Contemporary Polish painting and sculpture housed in a former Jewish prayer house. (p113)

Galeria Dyląg Private gallery of modern works from the 1940s to the 1970s. (p74)

Galeria Plakatu Beautifully crafted film posters stuffed into every nook and cranny. (p74)

Jewish Heritage

Kraków, more particularly Kazimierz, was an important centre of Jewish life for centuries. This cultural vibrancy vanished overnight, due to the mass deportation and extermination of the Jews at the hands of the Germans during WWII. This legacy has left the city with Central Europe's most important collection of Jewish heritage sights.

AGSAZ / SHUTTERSTOCK ©

Best Museums

Galicia Jewish Museum Both commemorates Jewish victims of the Holocaust and celebrates the Jewish culture and history of the region of Galicia. (p78)

Old Synagogue The synagogue dates from the 15th century and houses an exhibition on Jewish liturgical objects. (p86)

Schindler's Factory Interactive museum covers the Nazi occupation of Kraków in WWII, housed in the former enamel factory of Oskar Schindler. (p102)

Pharmacy Under the Eagle This exhibition in a former pharmacy tells the story of owner Tadeusz Pankiewicz, who risked his life trying to help Jewish residents in WWII. (p107)

Best Synagogues

High Synagogue Built around 1560, this is the third-oldest synagogue in Kraków after the Old and Remuh Synagogues. (p87)

Remuh Synagogue The area's smallest synagogue and one of only a couple regularly used for religious services. (p88)

Isaac Synagogue Kraków's largest synagogue has been restored and now houses an exhibition titled 'In Memory of Polish Jews'. (pictured; p88)

Best Other Sights

Remuh Cemetery Tiny burial ground situated just off of ul Szeroka in Kazimierz. The cemetery was mostly spared damage by the Nazis during WWII. (p86)

New Jewish Cemetery Highly moving burial ground that holds some 9000 tombstones, testifying to the former size of the Jewish quarter. (p129)

Jewish Literature

Try the **Austeria bookshop** in Kazimierz for an excellent selection of Jewish and Holocaust literature in English, plus posters and music CDs. (p99)

For Kids

Poles are family-oriented, and there are plenty of activities for children around the city. An increasing number of restaurants cater specifically to children, with play areas, and many offer a children's menu. Kids normally pay half price for attractions up to age 15 (under five free) and young children ride free on public transport.

AGNES KANTARUK / SHUTTERSTOCK ©

Best Hands-On Learning

Museum of Municipal Engineering Stuffed with trams and trucks, as well as some hands-on magnetic and water experiments. (pictured; p89)

Stanisław Lem Science Garden An outdoor garden filled with clever exhibits that teach the natural properties of optics, mechanics and acoustics. (p129)

MICET Aimed at budding actors and theatre directors and encourages kids to design their own sets and costumes. (p64)

Best Outdoor Activities

Jordan Park Lots of playgrounds and climbing frames, and a kid-friendly

ice skating rink from December to March. (p118)

Krakowski Park Following a complete refresh, offers plenty of space for kids to run around or watch the swans. (p118)

Zoological Gardens Well-tended and filled with exotic animals, including elephants, hippos and a rare breed of horse. (p119

Best Rainy-Days

Rynek Underground Kids will be dazzled by the

holograms and audiovisual tricks. (p54)

History Land Will open up younger eyes with all the virtual-reality tech on hand – and the exhibits are built from LEGO blocks. (p130)

Park Wodny This water park has it all: pools, slides, saunas and, yeah, hot tubs. Parents have to have fun too. (p131)

Top Tips

○ Look for the handy brochure *Kids in Kraków* (www.kidsinkrakow.pl) at Info Kraków tourist offices.

○ There are nappy-changing facilities in newer museums and in shopping malls like **Galeria Krakowska**, near the train station. (p145)

Festivals & Events

Kraków has one of the richest cycles of annual events in Poland. Indeed, the summer months are crammed with overlapping festivals to the point where even locals say there might be too much of a good thing. For information head to a branch of the InfoKraków tourist office or check online at the Kraków Festival Guide (www.krakowfestival.com).

NURPHOTO / CONTRIBUTOR / GETTY IMAGES ©

Best for Music

Shanties (International Festival of Sailors' Songs; www.shanties.pl; ☺Feb) Brings boisterous sailors' songs to bars and halls around town.

Unsound (www.unsound. pl; ☺Oct) A week of experimental music, installations and related visual arts.

Wianki (www.wianki.krakow.pl; ☺Jun) Boisterous midsummer night concert held outdoors along the Vistula River.

Best Religious & Cultural Events

Juvenalia (www.juwenalia. krakow.pl; ☺May) Annual carnival where students receive symbolic keys to the town's gates.

Jewish Culture Festival (www.jewishfestival. pl; ☺late Jun–early Jul; pictured) Ten days of Jewish arts and culture, theatre, film and music.

Kraków Christmas Crib Competition (www. szopki.eu; ☺Dec) Annual competition pits crib against crib on the Main Market Square.

Lajkonik Pageant (www. mhk.pl; ☺May or Jun) Colourful spring pageant headed by the 'Lajkonik', a comic figure disguised as a bearded Tatar.

Best for Theatre & Film

Film Music Festival (www.fmf.fm; ☺May) Annual festival dedicated to film music and soundtracks.

Kraków Film Festival (www.kff.com.pl; ☺late May–early Jun) Brings hundreds of films from around the world to local audiences.

International Festival of Street Theatre (www. teatrkto.pl; ☺Jul) Performances, circus, dance and music around the Old Town.

Best for Literature

Miłosz Festival (www. miloszfestival.pl; ☺Jun) Dedicated to late Polish poet and Nobel laureate Czesław Miłosz.

Conrad Festival (www. conradfestival.pl; ☺Oct) International literary festival inspired by, but not limited to, the works of Polish writer Joseph Conrad.

Tours

Many companies offer guided tours of the city or of particular neighbourhoods. These usually involve walking, but tours on bus, bike and golf cart are common. A guided tour also makes good sense for day-trip destinations like the Wieliczka Salt Mine, as the tour company can sort out travel and ticketing logistics.

SANTI RODRIGUEZ / SHUTTERSTOCK ©

Best General Sightseeing Tours

Cracow City Tours Decent range of walking and bus tours, including a popular four-hour coach tour, as well as longer excursions to the Wieliczka Salt Mine and Auschwitz-Birkenau Memorial and Museum. (p120)

SeeKrakow The largest tour operator in Kraków offers a bewildering array of tours, including of Schindler's Factory and the Rynek Underground. (p131)

WowKrakow! Popular 'Hop-On Hop-Off' bus that allows passengers to stop at their leisure at 15 different areas of interest around town. (p130)

Best Walking (& Crawling) Tours

Free Walking Tour Free walking tours provided by licensed guides who make their money from tips. Old Town tours depart six times daily from March to October (shorter hours November to February). (p65)

Kraków Pub Crawl Classic drinking tour visits four venues and starts out from the Main Market Square in front of the **Adam Mickiewicz Statue**. (p66)

Cracovia Walking Tours Two-hour walking tours conducted by licensed guides through the Old Town. (p65)

Best Special-Interest Tours

Cool Tour Company A four-hour spin around town on two wheels that departs twice daily from May to September at 10am and 3pm. (p65)

Jarden Tourist Agency Mainly Jewish-themed tours, including two- and three-hour walking tours of Kraków's Kazimierz and Podgórze. (p90)

Pictured: St Mary's Basilica (p52), Old Town

Four Perfect Days

Day 1

Start at the **Main Market Square** (p59). See the square from above at the **Town Hall Tower** (p41) or below at the **Rynek Underground** (p54). Explore the **Cloth Hall** (p62) and hear the bugler's call from **St Mary's Basilica** (p52).

After lunch at **Hawełka** (p68), stop by the **Museum of Pharmacy** (p62) and **Czartoryski Museum** (p62) to see Da Vinci's *Lady With an Ermine*. Cross the square to visit **Collegium Maius** (pictured; p56), where Copernicus studied.

Stay in the Old Town for dinner at **Cyrano de Bergerac** (p66) or **Wentzl** (p67). Afterward, head to **Harris Piano Jazz Bar** (p72) for music or **Pauza** (p71) or **Spokój** (p70) for drinks.

Day 2

Get an early start to visit **Wawel Royal Castle** (p36). See the **Royal Private Apartments** and **State Rooms** and check out **Wawel Cathedral** (pictured). Before lunch, pop into the **Basilica of St Francis** (p43) to admire the stained glass.

After lunching at **Miód Malina** (p46) or **Restauracja Pod Baranem** (p90), walk over to **Kazimierz**. Amble around, taking in former synagogues like the **High Synagogue** (p87) and **Old Synagogue** (p86). Don't miss the **Galicia Jewish Museum** (p78).

Continue the Jewish theme with dinner at **Dawno Temu Na Kazimierzu** (p91) and stay in Kazimierz for drinks and fun. Good bets are **Mleczarnia** (p96) and **Hevre** (p95).

Day 3

ALEXEY PEVNEY / SHUTTERSTOCK ©

Make your way to **Schindler's Factory** (pictured; p102) to learn about the German occupation. Art lovers will love the **Museum of Contemporary Art in Kraków** (p108). The **Pharmacy Under the Eagle** (p107) nearby is worth seeing.

After lunch at **ZaKładka Food & Wine** (p109), spend the day west of the Old Town. Visit the **National Museum** (p118) or explore glass painting at the **Stained Glass Workshop & Museum** (p118). Feeling ambitious? **Kościuszko Mound** (p118) is a rewarding side trip.

For dinner and afterwards, take a spin through the **Tytano** complex and its hip clubs. **Veganic** (p121) is good for food, then head over for beers at **Weźże Krafta** (p123) or dancing at **Scena54** (p123).

Day 4

KANUMAN / GETTY IMAGES ©

The last day requires a choice: **Auschwitz-Birkenau Memorial & Museum** (p136) or **Wieliczka Salt Mine** (pictured; p140)? You won't have time for both. If you start early, you can visit the mine before lunch and spend rest of the day in Kraków.

Many Wieliczka tour buses drop you at **Glonojad** (p121), an excellent spot for lunch. After eating, hop the tram to the workers' community of **Nowa Huta**. Highlights include its 1950s Socialist-Realist architecture and the **Museum of the People's Republic of Poland** (p135).

For dinner, splurge at **Art Restaurant** (p45) or **Pod Aniołami** (p46), stroll the **Planty** (p72) and finish at **Bunkier Cafe** (p69).

Need to Know
For detailed information, see Survival Guide p143

Currency
Polish złoty (zł)

Language
Polish

Visas
EU citizens do not need visas and can stay indefinitely. Citizens of many other countries can stay for up to 90 days without a visa.

Money
ATMs are ubiquitous. Credit cards are generally accepted and often preferred to cash.

Mobile Phones
GSM and 4G networks are available through inexpensive SIM cards.

Time
Central European Time (GMT/UTC plus one hour)

Tipping
In restaurants and cafes, for smaller tabs round the bill to the nearest 5zł or 10zł increment. Otherwise, 10% is standard.

Daily Budget

Budget: Less than 250zł
Dorm beds: 45–90zł
Excellent supermarkets for self-catering: 50–70zł
Herring and a shot of vodka: 15–20zł

Midrange: 250–650zł
Double room at midrange hotel: 300–450zł
Dinner with starter and wine: 110–130zł
Museum admission: 20zł

Top End: More than 650zł
Double room at luxury hotel: 500–800zł
Four-course dinner at top restaurant: 265zł
Best seat at the opera: 200zł

Advance Planning

Three months before Book your hotel room, especially if you're travelling during summer or over the Easter and Christmas holidays.

One month before Buy tickets online for popular attractions such as Wawel Royal Castle (pictured right), Schindler's Factory and Rynek Underground. Check Karnet Kraków (www.karnet.krakow.pl) for what's on.

One week before Arrange a tour of Wieliczka Salt Mine. Reserve tables at better restaurants.

Arriving in Kraków

Most visitors arrive via Kraków John Paul II International Airport or the Main Train Station (Kraków Główny) or Bus Station.

✈ Kraków John Paul II International Airport

Around 30 minutes drive west of the Old Town.

Train Special Airport trains (9zł) connect the airport with Kraków's Main Station.

Bus City bus 208 (4.60zł) runs to Kraków's Bus Station.

Taxi A taxi to the centre costs from 70zł to 90zł and takes 30 minutes.

🚋 Main Train & Bus Stations

The train and bus stations are adjacent. Both are a 10-minute walk north of the Old Town.

Tram Find tram stops outside the train station. Handy for reaching places in Kazimierz and Podgórze,

Taxi Usually the easiest way of reaching your hotel on arrival.

Getting Around

The centre is compact and walking is the best way to move around the Old Town or between the Old Town and Wawel Hill.

🚋 Tram

The network is dense, and trams are a good option for moving between the Old Town and Kazimierz and Podgórze.

🚌 Bus

Buses are aimed more at commuters, though there are a few attractions best reached by bus.

🚲 Bike

Cyclists encounter lots of cars and trams, though officials continue to build out the trail infrastructure.

🚖 Taxi

Convenient for rides back to the hotel and airport transfers.

Kraków Neighbourhoods

Old Town (p51)

The centre of Kraków life since the Tatar invasions of the 13th century, the Old Town, with its graceful Main Market Square (Rynek Główny), is filled with historical buildings and monuments.

Wawel Hill & Around (p35)

Wawel Hill, south of the Old Town, is the silent guardian of a millennium of Polish history. The hilltop castle was the seat of kings and queens from the earliest days of the Polish state.

John Paul II Kraków-Balice International ✈ *(12.5km)*
←

Western Kraków (p115)

Western Kraków is the prim and prosperous side of town, filled with tidy streets that are lined with well-maintained 19th- and early-20th-century townhouses.

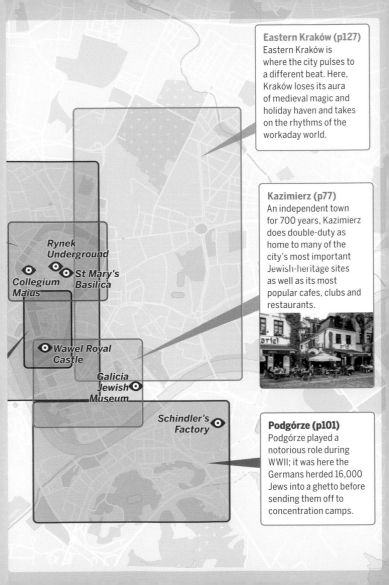

Eastern Kraków (p127)
Eastern Kraków is where the city pulses to a different beat. Here, Kraków loses its aura of medieval magic and holiday haven and takes on the rhythms of the workaday world.

Kazimierz (p77)
An independent town for 700 years, Kazimierz does double-duty as home to many of the city's most important Jewish-heritage sites as well as its most popular cafes, clubs and restaurants.

Podgórze (p101)
Podgórze played a notorious role during WWII; it was here the Germans herded 16,000 Jews into a ghetto before sending them off to concentration camps.

Rynek Underground

Collegium Maius

St Mary's Basilica

Wawel Royal Castle

Galicia Jewish Museum

Schindler's Factory

Explore
Kraków

Explore ◉
Wawel Hill
& Around

The symbol of a nation, Wawel Hill, south of the Old Town, is the silent guardian of a millennium of Polish history. The hilltop castle was the seat of kings and queens from the earliest days of the Polish state and the site of its most solemn ceremonies and most celebrated moments. Many Polish monarchs found their final resting place below Wawel Cathedral.

The Short List

○ **Wawel Royal Castle (p36)** *Touring the lavish state rooms and residences of Poland's kings and queens.*

○ **Wawel Cathedral (p38)** *Gawking at yet another gorgeous church, this one the main coronation – and burial – spot for Polish monarchs.*

○ **Church of SS Peter and Paul (p43)** *Noting the contrast between the church's elaborate baroque exterior and its sober interior.*

○ **Basilica of St Francis (p43)** *Smiling at all of those playful art nouveau stained-glass windows.*

○ **Bishop Erazm Ciołek Palace (p44)** *Appreciating the simple beauty of early Christian artwork from the 12th and 13th centuries.*

Getting There & Around

🚊 Routes 6, 8, 10, 13 and 18 drop you near Wawel Castle.

🚊 Routes 1, 6, 8, 13, 18 bisect the Old Town and are good for reaching ul Grodzka.

Wawel Hill Map on p42

View over Kraków to Wawel Royal Castle (p36)

Top Sight 📷
Wawel Royal Castle

Any trip to Kraków inevitably involves a trek up stately Wawel Hill to pay respects to the former seat of the Polish monarchy. Even if you don't plan on entering the paid attractions, it's worth the effort. The grounds are free to enter, and the scale, architecture and exuberant atmosphere – usually infused with the laughter of school kids – are impressive.

◎ **MAP P42, B5**

Zamek Królewski na Wawelu

www.wawel.krakow.pl

Wawel Hill

🚋 6, 8, 10, 13, 18

State Rooms

The largest and most impressive exhibition at Wawel Castle are these 20 or so chambers that have been restored to their original Renaissance and early-baroque style and crammed with period furnishings and works of art. The **Hall of Senators** houses a magnificent series of 16th-century Arras tapestries following the story of Adam and Eve, Cain and Abel, or Noah (they are rotated periodically). The **Hall of Deputies** has a fantastic coffered ceiling with 30 individually carved and painted wooden heads.

Royal Private Apartments

A visit to the Royal Private Apartments imparts great insight into how the other half (at least in the 16th century) once lived. You'll see plenty of magnificent old tapestries, mostly northern French and Flemish, hanging on the walls. Other highlights include the so-called Hen's Foot, Jadwiga's gemlike chapel in the northeast tower, and the sumptuous Gdańsk-made furniture in the Alchemy Room.

Crown Treasury & Armoury

The treasury and armoury are housed in vaulted Gothic rooms surviving from the 14th-century castle. The most famous object in the treasury is the *Szczerbiec* (Jagged Sword), dating from the mid-13th century, which was used at all Polish coronations from 1320 onward. The armoury features a collection of old weapons from various epochs, including crossbows, swords, lances and halberds.

Lost Wawel

Located in the old royal kitchen, this exhibition features the very oldest treasures up here, including remnants of the late-10th-century **Rotunda of SS Felix and Adauctus**, reputedly

★ Top Tips

o Note the attractions at Wawel Castle must be booked and paid for separately.

o Don't feel you have to see everything to have 'done' the castle. Instead, pick one or two attractions and focus your visit on those.

o The **Wawel Visitor Centre** (🖊guides 12 422 1697, info 12 422 5155; ⏰9am-8pm May-Aug, to 7pm Apr & Sep, to 6pm Mar & Oct, to 5pm Nov-Feb; 📶) can be a lifesaver. The harried but polite staff here can help plan your visit and book tours and tickets.

o Most of the attractions can only be seen by guided tour, which must be booked in advance.

✕ Take a Break

There's a cafe within the **Wawel Visitor Centre**. For something good and not far away from the entrance to the castle complex, try Miód Malina (p46).

the first church in Poland, as well as various archaeological finds and models of previous Wawel churches.

Wawel Cathedral

The **cathedral** (☎ 12 429 9515; www. katedra-wawelska.pl; admission free; ⏰ 9am-5pm Mon-Sat, from 12.30pm Sun Apr-Oct, to 4pm Nov-Mar) has been site of countless coronations, funerals and burials of Poland's monarchs and strongmen over the centuries – it's and suitably decked out. Highlights include the Holy Cross Chapel, Sigismund Chapel, Sigismund Bell and the Royal Crypts. Touring all of these could take the whole afternoon, but try not to miss the crypts, where a who's who of Polish royalty and power are buried.

Wawel Cathedral Museum

Diagonally opposite the cathedral is this **treasury** (☎ 12 429 9515; www. katedra-wawelska.pl; adult/concession 12/7zł; ⏰ 9am-5pm Mon-Sat) of historical and religious objects from the cathedral. There are plenty of exhibits, including church plates and royal funerary regalia, but not a single crown. They were all apparently stolen from the treasury by the Prussians in 1795 and reputedly melted down.

Dragon's Den

If you've had enough of high art and baroque furnishings, complete your Wawel trip with a visit to the cheesy Dragon's Den, former home of the legendary **Wawel Dragon** and an easy way to get down from

Holy Cross Chapel, Wawel Cathedral

Seat of Polish Kings & Queens

The buildings on Wawel Hill constitute the most significant architectural collection in Poland.

The Early Centuries

There's been a royal building here for the better part of 1000 years. The first significant structures date from the 11th century and were commissioned by King Bolesław I Chrobry. His relatively small residence was given a big Gothic makeover in the 14th century, though much of that castle burned down in 1499. Soon after, King Zygmunt I Stary commissioned a new residence in the then-fashionable Renaissance style.

No Longer Royal

Once the Polish capital was transferred to Warsaw at the end of the 16th century, the Wawel buildings lost something of their raison d'être, though coronations and celebrations continued to take place. The grounds were repeatedly sacked by marauding Swedish and Prussian armies in the 17th and 18th centuries, and the castle was occupied in the 19th century by the Austrians.

Wawel After Independence

After Kraków was incorporated into the re-established Poland after WWI, Wawel became a residence of the Polish president. During WWII, Wawel again assumed its historic role, but this time far more reluctantly. Kraków became the capital of German-occupied Poland, with Wawel serving as the residence for Nazi Governor General Hans Frank.

Wawel Hill. The entrance to the cave is next to the **Thieves' Tower** (Baszta Złodziejska) at the southwestern end of the complex. From here you'll have a good panorama over the Vistula and the suburbs further west.

Exhibition of Oriental Art

The Exhibition of Oriental Art comprises a collection of 17th-century Turkish banners and weaponry, captured after the Battle of Vienna and displayed along with a variety of old Persian carpets, Chinese and Japanese ceramics, and other Asian antiques.

Walking Tour 🚶

Route of Kings & Queens

This walk hits many of Kraków's highlights and follows the old coronation route of Poland's kings and queens. It pays respects to the main attractions in a relatively logical path, beginning in the Old Town and wending its way out to Wawel Hill.

Walk Facts

Start Florian Gate
End Wawel Royal Castle
Length 2km; two hours

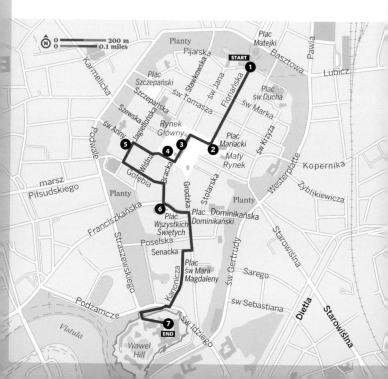

❶ Kraków's Main Gate

Start at the **Florian Gate** (www.muzeumkrakowa.pl; ul Floriańska; ⊙10.30am-6pm Apr-Oct; adult/concession 9/7zł; 🚋2, 4, 14, 18, 20, 24, 44), an attractive stone gateway built around 1300. It was once the city's main entryway and is the only one of its original eight gates still standing.

❷ St Mary's Basilica

Continue down lively ul Floriańska. To your left as you enter the Main Market Square is twin-spired St Mary's Basilica (p52). Arrive on the hour to hear the bugler play from the taller tower.

❸ Renaissance Perfection

Dominating the centre of the square is the lively Cloth Hall (p62), a two-level Renaissance confection that serves many purposes, including as the entryway to the Rynek Underground.

❹ Tower Without a Town Hall

The **Town Hall Tower** (Wieża Ratuszowa; 📞12 426 4334; www.muzeumkrakowa.pl; Rynek Główny 1; adult/concession 10/8zł; ⊙10.30am-6pm Apr-Oct; 🚋1, 6, 8, 13, 18), next door, recalls what must have been a glorious 15th-century building before the occupying Austrians dismantled it in the 19th century. You can still see the original Gothic portal.

❺ Ancient Centre of Learning

The Collegium Maius (p56) was the earliest home of Jagiellonian University, the second-oldest university in Central Europe. Pop in to the courtyard to see original Gothic portals and the famous clock.

❻ Art Nouveau Beauty

Many say the Basilica of St Francis (p43), a 13th-century Gothic beauty, is their favourite church because of the beautiful stained-glass windows by art nouveau master Stanisław Wyspiański. The most famous window, above the rear entrance, depicts God in the act of creation.

❼ The King Comes Home

Continue south on ul Grodzka, the final stage of the Royal Route, as far as ul Senacka, then turn south onto charming ul Kanonicza. This leads to the foot of Wawel Royal Castle (p36).

Franciszkańska

Plac
Wszystkich
Świętych

Basilica of **2**
St Francis

Plac
Dominikański

Dominikańska

21

15

OLD TOWN

Grodzka

23

14 Poselska

12

10

17

11

Poselska

5

Archaeological
Museum

Senacka

18

13

19

Kanonicza

Church of
SS Peter & Paul

1 **22**

9

4

Bishop Erazm
Ciołek Palace **3**

Church of
St Andrew

Grodzka

6

Archdiocesan
Museum

20

Trałowska

Planty

Planty

25

24

Straszewskiego

KLEPARZ

Podzamcze

7

św Idziego

**Wawel Royal
Castle**

Wawel
Hill

św Gertrudy

Droga do Zamku

Stradomska

Bernardyńska

KAZIMIERZ

16

8

For reviews see	
◉ Top Sights	p36
◎ Sights	p43
✕ Eating	p45
🍷 Drinking	p48
✪ Entertainment	p49
🔒 Shopping	p49

0   100 m
0   0.05 miles

Sights

Church of SS Peter & Paul CHURCH

1 MAP P42, D3

The Jesuits erected this church, the first baroque building in Kraków, after they had been brought to the city in 1583 to do battle with supporters of the Reformation. Designed on the Latin cross layout and topped with a large skylit dome, the church has a refreshingly sober interior, apart from some fine stucco decoration on the vault. (✆12 350 6365; www.apostolowie.pl; ul Grodzka 52a; ◷9am-5pm Tue-Sat, 1.30-5pm Sun; ▥6, 8, 10, 13, 18)

Basilica of St Francis CHURCH

2 MAP P42, B1

Duck into the dark basilica on a sunny day to admire the artistry of Stanisław Wyspiański, who designed the fantastic art nouveau stained-glass windows. The multicoloured deity in the chancel above the organ loft is a masterpiece. From the transept, you can also enter the Gothic cloister of the Franciscan Monastery to admire the fragments of 15th-century frescoes. Closed to tourists during mass. (Bazylika Św Franciszka; ✆12 422 5376; www.franciszkanska.pl; Plac Wszystkich Świętych 5; ◷10am-4pm Mon-Sat, from 1pm Sun; ▥1, 6, 8, 13, 18)

Basilica of St Francis

DAVID CLAPP / GETTY IMAGES ©

Bishop Erazm Ciołek Palace
MUSEUM

3 👁 MAP P42, C3

Quaint Kanonicza is the perfect street to put a palace and fill it with age-old paintings and sculptures. This newish branch of the National Museum contains two exhibits of religious artwork. The Art of Old Poland (12th to 18th centuries) includes loads of Gothic paintings, altar pieces and a room devoted to sculptor Veit Stoss. A second exhibit focuses on Orthodox art. (📞12 433 5920; www.mnk.pl; ul Kanonicza 17; adult/concession 10/5zł; 🕙9am-4pm Tue-Fri, 10am-6pm Sat, 10am-4pm Sun; 🚊6, 8, 10, 13, 18)

Church of St Andrew
CHURCH

4 👁 MAP P42, D3

This church is almost a thousand years old. Built towards the end of the 11th century, much of its austere Romanesque stone exterior has been preserved. As soon as you enter, though, you're in a totally different world; its small interior was subjected to a radical baroque overhaul in the 18th century. (📞12 422 1612; ul Grodzka 54; 🕙8am-6pm Mon-Fri; 🚊6, 8, 10, 13, 18)

Archaeological Museum
MUSEUM

5 👁 MAP P42, B2

You can learn about the Małopolska region's history from the Palaeolithic period up until the early Middle Ages here, but you'll be most enthralled by the collection of ancient Egyptian artefacts, including both human and animal mummies. There are also more than 4000 iron coins from the 9th century. The gardens are a lovely place for a stroll. (📞12 422 7560; www.ma.krakow.pl; ul Poselska 3; adult/concession 12/7zł, free Sun; 🕙9am-3pm Mon, Wed & Fri, to 6pm Tue & Thu, 11am-4pm Sun; 🚊1, 6, 8, 13, 18)

Archdiocesan Museum
MUSEUM

6 👁 MAP P42, C4

This collection of religious sculpture and paintings, dating from the 13th to 16th centuries, is located in a 14th-century townhouse. Also on display is the room where Karol Wojtyła (the late Pope John Paul II) lived from 1958 to 1967, complete with his furniture and belongings – including his skis. There's a treasury of gifts he received here too. (Muzeum Archidiecezjalne; 📞12 421 8963; www.archimuzeum.pl; ul Kanonicza 19-21; adult/concession 10/6zł; 🕙10am-5pm Tue-Sun; 🚊6, 8, 10, 13, 18)

Ster
CRUISE

7 👁 MAP P42, A4

One-hour river tours of Kraków landmarks and longer five-hour trips out to the Benedictine Abbey in Tyniec aboard the *Peter Pan* or *Sobieski* – the longer trip allows for a one-hour stop at the abbey before turning around. Reserve tickets online or by phone. The departure point is not far from the Dębnicki Bridge, below the Sheraton Kraków hotel, and accessed

'Smok' the Magic Dragon

Wawel Castle is home to the city's oldest legends, including at least one involving a fire-breathing dragon. Long ago, the story goes, during Prince Krak's reign, a nasty dragon lived in the cave below Wawel Hill, terrorising Kraków town. A fire-breathing menace, the scaly Smok ravaged residents and livestock, leaving death and destruction in his wake. His favourite food was beautiful young virgins.

Prince Krak feared for the life of his own daughter Wanda, and he offered her hand in marriage to any suitor who could slay the dragon. Many died trying. Finally, a poor young cobbler came up with a scheme to trick the dragon. He stuffed a sheep with sulphur and left the tasty morsel outside the dragon's lair. The dragon fell for it.

The dragon devoured the sheep, then retreated to the Vistula River to quench his unbearable thirst. He drained the river, causing his stomach to swell and inciting a massive explosion. The dragon was defeated! The cobbler was a hero! The virgins were safe! And Wanda and the cobbler lived happily ever after.

from ul Zwierzyniecka. (☏601 560 250; www.rejsykrakow.com; cruise 1hr adult/concession 40/30zł, 5hr 85/70zł; ☺10am-6pm May-Oct; ﹢; ☐1, 2, 6)

Statek Nimfa
CRUISE

 8 ⊙ MAP P42, A6

The pleasure boat *Nimfa* cruises along the Vistula River, departing from the pier below Wawel Royal Castle, and motoring past sights such as Kościuszko Mound, Skałka and Plac Bohaterów Getta, with up-close views of all six bridges. The four-hour tour goes all the way to Tyniec. Reserve tickets online or by phone. (☏12 422 0855; www.statekkrakow.com; Wawel Pier; cruise 1hr adult/concession 40/30zł, 4hr 85/70zł; ☺10am-6pm May-Oct; ﹢; ☐6, 8, 10, 13, 18)

Eating

Art Restaurant
POLISH $$$

9 ✖ MAP P42, C3

Easily the most ambitious restaurant in this part of town, the Art is all white linens and swish service, but forget any notion of fusty food. The menu highlights farm-fresh ingredients and local sourcing, with plenty of unusual touches like red-pepper jam served with lamb saddle. Book on the terrace in nice weather. The lunch menu is great value (69zł). (Art Restauracja; ☏537 872 193; www.artrestauracja.com; ul Kanonicza 15; mains 60-90zł, seven-/nine-course tasting menu 239/289zł; ☺1-10pm; ☏; ☐6, 8, 10, 13, 18)

Black Duck

POLISH $$$

10 MAP P42, D2

The duck meat at this restaurant arrives specially from Poznań, and good use is made of it. From duck pierogi to duck soup with meatballs, as well as a whole roasted duck for two, this twist on Polish cuisine offers fine dining and an amazing array of dishes. Try the three-course vodka tasting (from 14zł) to get things moving. (Czarna Kaczka; ☎12 426 5440; www.facebook.com/CzarnaKaczka; ul Poselska 22; mains 45-90zł; ⏱noon-11pm; 📶; 🚃1, 6, 8, 13, 18)

Miód Malina

POLISH $$$

11 MAP P42, C2

The charmingly named Honey Raspberry serves high-quality Polish cooking in colourful surrounds.

Grab a window seat and order the wild mushrooms in cream, and any of the duck or veal dishes. There's a variety of beef steaks on the menu as well. The grilled sheep's-cheese appetiser, served with cranberry jelly, is a regional speciality. Reservations essential. (☎12 430 0411; www.miodmalina.pl; ul Grodzka 40; mains 40-80zł; ⏱noon-11pm; 📶; 🚃1, 6, 8, 13, 18)

Pod Aniołami

POLISH $$$

12 MAP P42, C2

This is the quintessential old Kraków restaurant; its main dining room occupies a Gothic cellar from the 13th century. Heavy wood furniture, stone walls and fraying tapestries evoke the Middle Ages, as do the grilled meats cooked over a beech-wood fire. The wild

Pod Aniołami

boar steak marinated in juniper berry comes highly recommended. (📞12 421 3999; www.podaniolami.pl; ul Grodzka 35; mains 45-80zł; ⏰1pm-midnight; 📶; 🚋1, 6, 8, 13, 18)

Bar Grodzki
POLISH $

13 ✖ MAP P42, C2

A delightful, family-run *bar mleczny* (milk bar), but a slight step up from the typical cafeteria setting. Line up at the steam table and choose your food. Highlights include a range of coleslaws, classic Polish mains like stuffed cabbage rolls and delicious *kompot* (juice of stewed fruit). (📞12 422 6807; www.grodzkibar.zaprasza.net; ul Grodzka 47/4; mains 10-20zł; ⏰9am-7pm Mon-Sat, from 10am Sun; 🚾; 🚋1, 6, 8, 13, 18)

Corse
MEDITERRANEAN $$

14 ✖ MAP P42, D2

This Corsican restaurant serves one of the more unusual cuisines available in Kraków. Its nautical decor, with white-canvas sail material hanging from the ceiling, feels upscale but comfortable, and the dishes – baked sea bass, duck magret, leg of lamb – are well prepared. (📞12 421 6273; www.corserestaurant.pl; ul Poselska 24; mains 40-70zł; ⏰1-11pm; 📶; 🚋1, 6, 8, 13, 18)

Smak Ukraiński
UKRAINIAN $

15 ✖ MAP P42, C1

This countrified oasis, perched on one of the city's busiest pedestrian

Great Area for Food

Wawel Hill has some of the nicest restaurants in the city, though the quality usually comes with a price. There's a string of great places along ul Grodzka and on ul Poselska, which runs off ul Grodzka. Quiet ul Kanonicza offers a swish, exclusive location and restaurants here tend to be both good and pricey.

thoroughfares, presents authentic Ukrainian dishes in a cosy dining room, decorated with predictably folksy flair. Expect lots of dumplings, borscht (the Ukrainian variety) and waiters in waistcoats. (📞12 421 9294; www.ukrainska.pl; ul Grodzka 21; mains 22-30zł; ⏰noon-10.30pm; 🚋1, 6, 8, 13, 18)

Gate of India
INDIAN $$

16 ✖ MAP P42, D6

This handy Indian, located between Wawel and Kazimierz, is good value and a nice change of pace from milder Polish cooking. The spicy dishes are served with a dried chilli, coriander and fresh ginger and will have you going back for a second visit. Lots of vegetarian choices on the menu. Book in advance for Friday or Saturday dinner. (📞12 356 5563; www.gateofindia.pl; ul Stradomska 11; mains 25-40zł; ⏰noon-10pm, to 11pm Fri & Sat; 📶🚾; 🚋6, 8, 10, 13, 18)

Balaton

HUNGARIAN $$

17 ✕ MAP P42, C2

The Balaton has been standing here for as long as anyone can remember and evokes a certain nostalgia among residents. The waiters have been serving up the same mix of paprikas and goulash since communist days. A makeover has left it cleaner and nicer, but otherwise not much has changed. It's popular in the evening, so book in advance. (☎12 422 0469; www.balaton.krakow.pl; ul Grodzka 37; mains 25-40zł; ◷noon-10pm, to 11pm Fri & Sat; 🛜; 🚋1, 6, 8, 13, 18)

Drinking

Dziórawy Kocioł

CAFE

18 ☕ MAP P42, C2

Harry Potter fans should head to this quaint basement cafe hidden away on ul Grodzka. It's aptly decorated from tip to toe with magical memorabilia, Hogwarts House flags and hand-drawn character sketches. There is some deliciously sweet Butter-beer on the menu, as well as lots of appropriately named cakes. (Leaky Cauldron; ☎12 422 5884; www.facebook.com/dziorawykociol; ul Grodzka 50/1; ◷9am-10pm; 🛜♿; 🚋1, 6, 8, 13, 18)

Cafe Pianola

CAFE

19 ☕ MAP P42, C2

Convenient corner pit-stop, between Wawel and the Old Town, for excellent coffee or wine. Though the pavement tables are tempting in nice weather, don't miss the chance to glimpse the Renaissance interiors, with their high, arched ceilings and – yes – piano to the side. (☎12 422 3252; www.cafepianola.pl; ul Senacka 7; ◷8.30am-1am, 10am-midnight Sun; 🛜; 🚋6, 8, 10, 13, 18)

Indalo Cafe

CAFE

20 ☕ MAP P42, A3

Indalo is a quaint spot, well hidden but just minutes from the centre. The cafe began life as an arts and crafts centre, and you can still buy handmade ornaments as you sip your coffee or sample the cheesecake and other sweets. Indalo also has accommodation in several rooms (from 200zł) located above the cafe, including an apartment with kitchenette suitable for longer stays. (Indalo Cafe & Rooms; ☎12 431 0091; http://cafeindalo.pl; ul Tarłowska 15; ◷8am-10pm, from 9am Sun; 🛜; 🚋1, 6, 8, 13, 18)

Prozak 2.0

CLUB

21 ☕ MAP P42, C1

A legend in its own time, this nightlife giant entices revellers into its labyrinth of passageways, nooks and crannies. It specialises in presenting international DJs. (☎731 695 341; www.facebook.com/pg/ProzakDwaZero; Plac Dominikański 6; ◷10.30pm-6am Tue-Sun; 🛜; 🚋1, 6, 8, 13, 18)

Amber, Amber & (More) Amber

Amber, otherwise known as 'Baltic gold', is fossilised tree resin, usually found on the shores of the Baltic Sea. When it's cut and buffed it makes for a beautiful semi-precious 'stone' in a ring, necklace or brooch, and Kraków has plenty of galleries with beautiful and original designs and settings. Make sure to look around as prices can vary considerably.

Entertainment

Church of SS Peter & Paul
CONCERT VENUE

22 ⭐ MAP P42, D3

Hosts evening concerts of Vivaldi, Bach, Chopin and Strauss throughout the week, performed by the Cracow Chamber Orchestra of St Maurice. Buy tickets at the door before the concert or at any InfoKraków tourist information office. (☑ 695 574 526; ul Grodzka 52a; tickets adult/concession 60/40zł; ⏰ 8pm; 🚋 1, 6, 8, 13, 18)

Shopping

Schubert World of Amber
JEWELLERY

23 🔒 MAP P42, C2

As the name implies, this is more than a shop, it's a celebration of all things amber. Even if you're not in the market to buy, it's certainly worth a peek in to see the amazing selection of amber necklaces, earrings, brooches and pendants. (☑ 12 430 2114; www.sukiennice. krakow.pl; ul Grodzka 38; ⏰ 9am-8pm; 🚋 1, 6, 8, 13, 18)

Kobalt Pottery & More
CERAMICS

24 🔒 MAP P42, C4

Sells eye-poppingly beautiful ceramic designs from the western Polish city of Bolesławiec. The dishes, plates and bowls are all hand-painted with a unique stamping and brush technique, and can be found in kitchens around the country. (☑ 798 380 431; www.facebook.com/kobalt. pottery; ul Grodzka 62; ⏰ 10am-7pm; 🚋 6, 8, 10, 13, 18)

Boruni Gallery
JEWELLERY

25 🔒 MAP P42, C4

If you are curious to know more about amber, also known as Baltic gold, swing by this spacious gallery to watch the informative video about the various types of amber and its production processes. Beware the hard sell! (☑ 12 428 5086; www.boruni.pl; ul Grodzka 60; ⏰ 9am-9pm; 🚋 6, 8, 10, 13, 18)

Explore
Old Town

The centre of Kraków life since the Tatar invasions of the 13th century, the Old Town, with its graceful Main Market Square (Rynek Główny), is filled with historical buildings and monuments. It's packed with restaurants, galleries and allegedly more bars per square metre than anywhere else in Europe. It's been a Unesco World Heritage Site since 1978 and largely car-free.

The Short List

o **St Mary's Basilica (p52)** *Staring at the lavish interiors and carved altarpieces of Kraków's most important church.*

o **Czartoryski Museum (p62)** *Admiring Leonardo Da Vinci's Lady With an Ermine and other works once the museum re-opens after a long renovation.*

o **Rynek Underground (p54)** *Poking around the mysterious medieval world that exists below the Main Market Square.*

o **Collegium Maius (p56)** *Taking in an array of rare scientific instruments available to Renaissance-era scientists for unravelling the mysteries of the solar system.*

o **Museum of Pharmacy (p62)** *Thanking your lucky stars that modern medicine has advanced beyond the vials and elixirs presented here.*

Getting There & Around

🚋 Routes 1, 6, 8, 13 and 18 serve the Main Market Square.

🚋 Routes 2, 4, 14, 18, 20, 24 and 44 run to the northern end of Old Town.

Old Town Map on p60

Main Market Square (p59) MARCIN_KADZIOLKA / GETTY IMAGES ©

Top Sight 📷
St Mary's Basilica

Overlooking the Main Market Square, this striking red-brick church is dominated by two towers of different heights. The original church, built in the 1220s, was destroyed during a Tatar raid, after which construction of the current basilica began. Tour the exquisite interior, with its carved wooden altarpiece, and climb the tower for excellent views. Don't miss the hourly bugle call.

◉ MAP P60, E4

Basilica of the Assumption of Our Lady

Plac Mariacki 5, Rynek Główny

adult/concession 10/5zł

🕐 11.30am-6pm Mon-Sat, from 2pm Sun

🚊 1, 6, 8, 13, 18

Wall Paintings

The first details you'll notice on entering the church are the elaborate and colourful wall paintings. Many of these paintings are the work of Jan Matejko, the 19th-century Polish master of realism, and harmonise beautifully with the intricacy of the high altar. Don't forget to look up: also noteworthy is the dazzling, star-flecked blue ceiling.

Stained-Glass Windows

The chancel, the chamber that surrounds the main altar, is illuminated by a series of magnificent stained-glass windows dating from the late-14th century. On the opposite side of the church, above the organ loft, is a fine art-nouveau stained-glass window by the early-modern masters Stanisław Wyspiański and Józef Mehoffer.

Carved Altarpiece

Measuring 13m high and 11m wide, the basilica's celebrated altarpiece is the country's largest and most important piece of medieval art. It took a decade for its maker, Veit Stoss, to complete the work before it was consecrated in 1489. The main scene represents the Assumption of the Virgin surrounded by the Apostles.

Tower

Be sure to listen for the bugler's call on the hour. The melody is as old as the church itself and is associated with many of the city's legends. If you'd like to see how the city looks from way up here, you can pay a separate admission to climb the 239 or so steps of the 82m-high tower.

★ Top Tips

○ The best place to hear the bugle call and to see the bugler in action is from the small courtyard in front of the Church of St Barbara (p64).

○ Worshippers enter through the main entrance on the southwestern side; tourists enter through the side door to the southeast.

○ Though the church is crammed with visitors, try to exercise discretion as there are people here to worship and not to sightsee.

✕ Take a Break

Magia Cafe Bar (☏12 426 4773; www.facebook.com/MagiaCafeBar; Plac Mariacki 3; ☺9-1am; ☏), just around the corner, is great for a pick-me-up coffee. In the afternoon, head over to nearby **Viva la Pinta** (☏12 378 97 22; ul Floriańska 13; ☺4pm-midnight Mon-Sat, from 2pm Sun; ☏; 🚊2, 4, 14, 18, 20, 24, 44) to find a hidden beer garden.

Top Sight 📷
Rynek Underground

This fascinating, high-tech attraction beneath the Main Market Square consists of an hour-long underground walk through medieval market stalls and other long-forgotten chambers. It's a kind of 'traditional archaeological museum meets modern-day interactive space' dedicated to telling the city's 1000-year history in a way that's interesting to visitors of all ages.

◎ MAP P60, D4

📞 12 426 5060

www.podziemiarynku.com

Rynek Główny 1

adult/concession 21/18zł, free Tue

🕙 10am-8pm Wed-Mon, to 4pm Tue

🚃 1, 6, 8, 13, 18

Audiovisual Delights

From the video images projected onto rising smoke that you see as you enter the underground, to the holograms and videos on display in the chambers, all the way to the documentary films on city life through the ages, the advanced technology employed here to tell Kraków's long story is a big part of the exhibition itself.

Early Kraków Life

The first part of the exhibition is given over to depictions of everyday life in the 13th and 14th centuries, with features on trade, transport and construction. Look for authentic paving stones from the 14th century as well as rebuilt dwellings of various craftsmen and traders. For the kids, there's a puppet show and a ghoulish re-creation of an 11th-century cemetery.

Model of the City

One of the highlights is an impressive scale model of the city in the 15th century near the height of its royal prowess, which shows the importance of the walls and the geographic relationship of the Old Town to Wawel Castle. In a nod to Paris, the model is illuminated by a pyramid-shaped skylight that juts into the surface of the square and can be seen from above ground.

Archaeological Finds

Serious museum buffs won't be disappointed, as much of the latter part of the exhibition route is dedicated to exploring various nooks and ruins uncovered during recent archaeological digs. On display here are the various tools and artefacts used over the years on the city's main square.

★ **Top Tips**

o Buy tickets at a special ticket office on the western side of the Cloth Hall (numbered Sukiennice 21).

o Note the electronic board at the office that shows tour times and the number of tickets available at each time.

o The actual entrance to the tunnels is on the opposite side of the Cloth Hall, on the northeastern end.

o Tuesdays are free, but you'll have to book well in advance since tickets are given out quickly.

✕ **Take a Break**

There's a **cafe** in the museum.

Noworolski (☏515 100 998; www. noworolski.com.pl; Rynek Główny 1/3; ⏱8.30am–midnight) is conveniently located next to the entrance to the Rynek Underground and a favourite for a coffee or a light meal.

Top Sight 📷
Collegium Maius

The Collegium Maius, built as part of the Kraków Academy (now the Jagiellonian University), is the oldest surviving university building in Poland, and one of the best examples of 15th-century Gothic architecture in the city. It has a magnificent arcaded courtyard (open from 7am to dusk) and a fascinating university collection.

◎ MAP P60, B4

www.maius.uj.edu.pl

ul Jagiellońska 15

adult/concession tour 16/12zł, exhibition 7/5zł

🕥 9am-2.20pm Mon-Fri, to 1.30pm Sat

🚊 2, 8, 13, 18, 20

Courtyard Clock

Even if you're not visiting the interior, it's worth peeking in on the picturesque, late-Gothic courtyard that dates from the 15th century. Be sure to time your visit to arrive at an odd hour between 9am and 3pm to see a short 16th-century spectacle of music and wooden figures who pop out through the windows below the courtyard clock.

Copernicus' Instruments

The tour passes through several historic interiors, with the most interesting being the displays of 15th- and 16th-century scientific equipment, including globes and telescopes of the kind that would have been used by one of the university's best-known alumni, Nicolaus Copernicus, who studied here in the 1490s. Also on display are some of Copernicus' manuscripts.

Jagiellonian Globe

There are plenty of paintings, sculptures, drawings and decorative arts on display – as well as a separate exhibition given over to medieval painting and visual arts. For most visitors the highlight of all of these curios will be the Jagiellonian Globe (dating from around 1510), which is the oldest known surviving globe to depict the American continent.

Aula

The original Renaissance ceiling here is crammed with portraits of kings, benefactors and rectors of the university (five of whom were sent off by the Germans to Sachsenhausen concentration camp in 1939). The treasury contains everything from copies of the 1364 university foundation papers and Jan III Sobieski's hammered silver table to an Oscar given to director Andrzej Wajda.

★ Top Tips

○ There is at least one tour in English each day, normally at 1pm (sometimes also at 11am).

○ In summer it's advisable to reserve in advance, either in person or by phone.

○ The courtyard can be entered free of charge.

○ At odd hours between 9am and 3pm the replica clock on the south side chimes and its cast of characters go through their paces.

✕ Take a Break

There's a decent **cafe** inside the museum.

If you're looking for something more substantial, try the Chimera Salad Bar (p67) – just around the corner from the main entrance.

Walking Tour 🥾

Historic Clubs & Cafes

Kraków's Main Market Square is one of Central Europe's liveliest public arenas. For centuries, though, it was not a tourist attraction, but rather the city's nerve centre and intellectual heart. While much of the modern-day square has been given over to visitors, there are venues still going strong here that remain near and dear to Cracovian hearts (and minds).

Walk Facts
Start Main Market Square
End Main Market Square
Length 1km; two hours

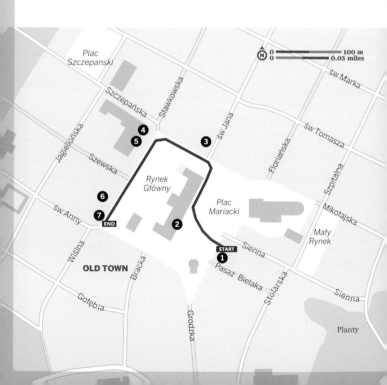

❶ Epic Club

Legendary Klub Pod Jaszczurami (p71) has been packing in students for happenings since the 1960s, and the black-and-white photos of performances through the years plastered on the walls testify to its pedigree. It's less vital these days, but peek inside and see the main stage, which still crackles with that old vibe.

❷ Political Favourite

Even if you don't stop for a coffee at Noworolski (p55), pause to admire the stunning art nouveau interiors by Polish artist Józef Mehoffer. The Noworolski has been here since 1910, serving the likes of Lenin and later becoming a favourite of occupying German officers. It feels timeless.

❸ Communist Classic

Clubs in Kraków come and go with the season, but steadfast Feniks (p71), located right on the main square, has survived and remains largely unchanged from communist days. The old-school decor is particularly evocative.

❹ Flapper Style

Chief among the charms at Europejska (p69) is the old-world atmosphere of the restaurant's back rooms. Striped wallpaper, green-velvet banquettes and gramophones lend a 1920s feel.

❺ Meet Gustav Klimt

The modest exterior of old-school Hawełka (p68) hides a world of late-19th-century art-nouveau splendour inside. You'll feel like you stepped back in time to the Austrian occupation before WWI.

❻ Rogues' Gallery

Vis-à-vis (p71), with its tiny stand-up bar, is famous for having the cheapest beer prices on the main square and for being a haunt of artists, painters, poets, singers and actors.

❼ Pub for the Ages

The Piwnica Pod Baranami (p72) (Under the Rams) harks back to the mid-1950s when it functioned as a 'literary cabaret'. Recent years have seen a calmer calendar, but it continues to host a summer jazz festival and other concerts and recitals throughout the year.

The Main Market Square

Measuring 200m by 200m, the **Main Market Square** (Rynek Główny; 🚋1, 6, 8, 13, 18) is the largest medieval square in Europe and one of the finest urban designs of its kind. Its layout, based on that of a *castrum* (Roman military camp), was drawn up in 1257 and has been retained to this day, though the buildings have changed over the centuries.

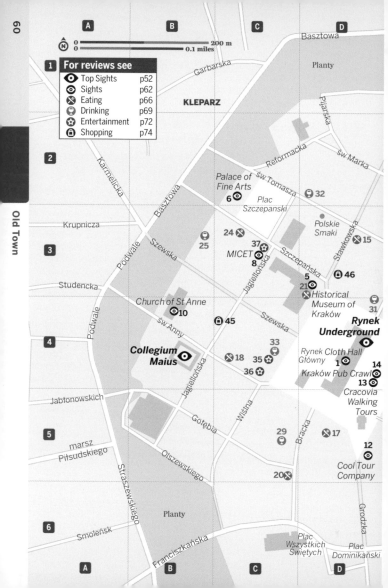

Old Town

For reviews see

- ◉ Top Sights   p52
- ◉ Sights   p62
- ✕ Eating   p66
- ❑ Drinking   p69
- ✿ Entertainment   p72
- ⬠ Shopping   p74

0 ———————— 200 m
0 ———————— 0.1 miles

Basztowa

Planty

Garbarska

KLEPARZ

Karmelicka

Reformacka

św. Marka

Pijarska

Krupnicza

Basztowa

św. Tomasza

Palace of
Fine Arts
6 ◉

Plac
Szczepanski

❑ 32

Polskie
Smaki

✕ 15

Podwale

Szewska

❑ 24 ✕
25

37 ✿
MICET
8 ◉

Szczepańska

Sławkowska

Studencka

Jagiellońska

Church of St Anne
◉**10**

🔒 **45**

5 ◉
21◉
✕ Historical
Museum of
Kraków

🔒 46

◉ 31

**Rynek
Underground**
◉

św. Anny

Szewska

Rynek Cloth Hall
Główny

1 ◉

14 ◉
13 ◉
Cracovia
Walking
Tours

**Collegium
Maius** ◉

✕ 18

33
❑
35 ✿
36 ✿

Kraków Pub Crawl◉

Jabłonowskich

Jagiellońska

Wiślna

Bracka

marsz
Piłsudskiego

Gołębia

29
❑

✕ 17

12
◉

Cool Tour
Company

Straszewskiego

Olszewskiego

20✕

Planty

Smoleńsk

Franciszkańska

Plac
Wszystkich
Świętych

Grodzka

Plac
Dominikański

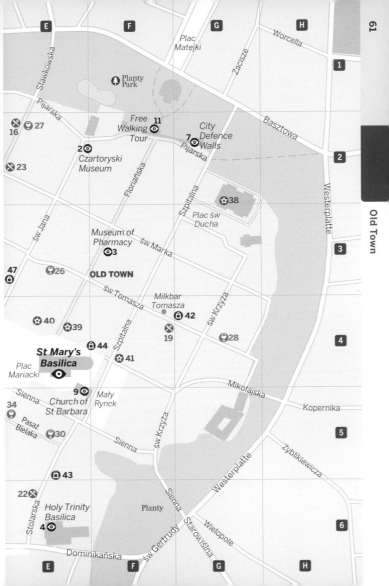

E
F
G
H

Worcella

1

Plac
Matejki

Zacisze

Planty
Park

Basztowa

Slawkowska

Pijarska

Free
Walking
Tour

11

City
Defence
Walls

2

Westerplatte

16
27

7

Pijarska

23

Czartoryski
Museum

Florianńska

Szpitalna

38

Plac św
Ducha

2

św. Jana

Museum of
Pharmacy
3

św. Marka

3

47

26

OLD TOWN

św Tomasza

Milkbar
Tomasza

42

28

40
39

Szpitalna

19

św. Krzyża

4

**St Mary's
Basilica**

44

41

Plac
Mariacki

9

Mały
Rynck

Mikołajska

Kopernika

Sienna
34

Church of
St Barbara

Pasaż
Bielaka
30

Sienna

św. Krzyża

Westerplatte

5

Zyblikiewicza

43

22

Holy Trinity
Basilica
4

Planty

Sienna

Starowiślna

Wielopole

6

Stolarska

Dominikańska

św. Gertrudy

E
F
G
H

Sights

Cloth Hall
HISTORIC BUILDING

1 ⊙ MAP P60, D4

Dominating the centre of the Main Market Square, this building was once the heart of Kraków's medieval clothing trade. Created in the early 14th century when a roof was put over two rows of stalls, it was extended into a 108m-long Gothic structure, then rebuilt in Renaissance style after a 1555 fire; the arcades were a late-19th-century addition. The ground floor is now a busy trading centre for crafts and souvenirs; the upper floor houses the **Gallery of 19th-Century Polish Painting.** (Sukiennice; Rynek Główny 1/3; admission free; 🚋1, 6, 8, 13, 18)

Czartoryski Museum
MUSEUM

2 ⊙ MAP P60, E2

The Czartoryski boasts the city's richest art collection, including Leonardo Da Vinci's 15th-century masterpiece, *Lady with an Ermine* (1489–90). Other exhibitions include Greek, Roman, Egyptian and Etruscan art as well as Turkish weaponry. The museum closed in 2010 for renovation and was set to reopen as a branch of the National Museum at the end of 2019. Until then, *Lady with an Ermine* is on display at the National Museum (p118) main branch. (📞12 370 5460; www.mnk.pl; ul Św Jana 19; 🚋2, 4, 14, 18, 20, 24, 44)

Museum of Pharmacy
MUSEUM

3 ⊙ MAP P60, F3

The name of this museum doesn't sound that exciting, but the Jagiellonian University Medical School's Museum of Pharmacy is one of the largest museums of its kind in Europe and arguably the best. Accommodated in a beautiful historic townhouse worth the visit alone, it features a 22,000-piece collection, which includes old laboratory equipment, rare pharmaceutical instruments, heaps of glassware, stoneware, mortars, jars, barrels, medical books and documents. (Muzeum Farmacji; 📞12 421 9279; www.muzeum.farmacja.uj.edu.pl; ul Floriańska 25; adult/concession 14/8zł; 🕙noon-6.30pm Tue, 9.30am-3pm Wed-Sun; 🚋2, 4, 14, 18, 20, 24, 44)

Holy Trinity Basilica
MONASTERY

4 ⊙ MAP P60, E6

Originally built in the 13th century, this massive church was badly damaged by fire in 1850. Note the original 14th-century doorway at the main (western) entrance to the church. The monastery, just behind the northern wall of the church, is accessible from the street (enter an unmarked door at Stolarska 12). Closed to tourists during Sunday mass. (Dominican Church; 📞12 423 1613; www.krakow. dominikanie.pl; ul Stolarska 12; admission free; 🕙9.30am-11.30am & 1.30pm-4.30pm; 🚋1, 6, 8, 13, 18)

Historical Museum of Kraków

MUSEUM

5 ⊙ MAP P60, D3

At the northern corner of the square, the collection within the 17th-century Krzysztofory Palace is home to Cyberteka, an interactive exhibition which charts the city from its earliest days to WWI. The museum features a bit of everything related to the city's past, including old clocks, armour, paintings, Kraków's celebrated *szopki* (Nativity scenes), and the costume of the Lajkonik. (Krzysztofory Palace; ☏12 619 2335; www.mhk. pl; Rynek Główny 35; adult/concession 12/8zł, free Sat; ⊘10am-5.30pm Tue-Sun; 🚊2, 4, 14, 18, 20, 24, 44)

Palace of Fine Arts

GALLERY

6 ⊙ MAP P60, C2

The centrepiece of the art nouveau Plac Szczepański is this elaborate edifice on its western side. An incredible frieze circles the building (product of Jacek Malczewski), while the busts on the facade honour Polish artists. The building is used for temporary art exhibits. (Pałac Sztuki; ☏12 422 6616; www. palac-sztuki.krakow.pl; Plac Szczepański 4; adult/concession 15/10zł; ⊘8.15am-6pm Mon-Fri, from 10am Sat & Sun; 🚊2, 4, 14, 18, 20, 24, 44)

City Defence Walls

HISTORIC SITE

7 ⊙ MAP P60, G2

This small museum includes entry to both the Florian Gate (p41) and **Barbican** (Barbakan; www.muzeum

Stalls in the Cloth Hall

krakowa.pl; ul Basztowa; adult/concession 9/7zł; ⏱10.30am-6pm Apr-Oct; 🚋2, 4, 14, 18, 20, 24, 44), among the few surviving remnants of the city's medieval defence walls. The Florian Gate was once the city's main entrance and dates from the 14th century. The Barbican, a circular bastion adorned with seven turrets, was built at the end of the 15th century to lend additional protection. It was once connected to the gate by a narrow passage running over a moat. (Mury Obronne; 📞12 421 1361; www.muzeumkrakowa.pl; ul Pijarska; adult/concession 9/7zł; ⏱10.30am-6pm May-Oct; 🚋2, 4, 14, 18, 20, 24, 44)

MICET
MUSEUM

8 ⊙ MAP P60, C3

MICET is something a little different. Situated in the Stary Theatre (p72), it's an interactive museum where visitors learn the traditional crafts associated with the theatre and then put their knowledge to use as they compose their own scenes, costumes and designs. It's kid-friendly and obviously best suited to visitors (of all ages) with an active interest in what happens backstage. (Muzeum Interaktywnym/Centrum Edukacji Teatralnej; 📞12 422 8020; www.micet.pl; ul Jagiellońska 1; adult/concession 12/8zł; ⏱11am-7pm Tue-Sun; 👫; 🚋2, 4, 14, 18, 20, 24, 44)

Church of St Barbara
CHURCH

9 ⊙ MAP P60, E5

This sombre 14th-century church is located on the small, charming Plac Mariacki, which was a churchyard until the early 19th century. St Barbara's was the cemetery chapel and served the Polish faithful during the Middle Ages. Note the skull and crossbones on the north exterior; just inside the entrance is an open chapel featuring stone sculptures of Christ and three of the Apostles, attributed to the Stoss school. (Kościół Św Barbary; 📞12 428 1500; www.swietabarbara.jezuici.pl; Plac Mariacki; ⏱8am-6pm; 🚋1, 6, 8, 13, 18)

Church of St Anne
CHURCH

10 ⊙ MAP P60, B4

Designed by Tylman van Gameren and built in the late-17th century as a university church, the Church of St Anne was long the site of inaugurations of the academic year, doctoral promotions and a resting place for many university professors and rectors. A spacious, stark-white interior fitted out with fine furnishings, gravestones and epitaphs, and embellished with superb stucco work and murals – all stylistically homogeneous – puts the church among the best classical baroque buildings in Poland. (Kościół Św Anny; 📞12 422 5318; www.kolegiata-anna.pl; ul Św Anny 11; ⏱8am-6pm; 🚋1, 6, 8, 13, 18)

Free Walking Tour
WALKING

11 ⊙ MAP P60, F2

These walking tours of the Old Town and Kazimierz are provided by licensed tour guides who make their money from tips. The Old

'Lady with an Ermine'

Kraków's most valuable work of art is doubtless Leonardo da Vinci's masterpiece *The Lady with an Ermine*. The painting, which was finished around 1490, is one of only a handful of portraits Leonardo made of women (another notable female portrait would be the *Mona Lisa*). The painting has had a remarkable history. It was stolen from Kraków by the Germans in WWII and returned by the American government after the war. For years, the work hung in the private collection of the Czartoryski family at the Czartoryski Museum (p62). In the past decade, though, the painting has bounced around various venues as the museum underwent a long and often-delayed renovation. At the end of 2019, the 'Lady' was set to return to the refurbished Czartoryski Museum, now part of the National Museum. Until the painting moves, it will hang at the main branch of the National Museum (p118).

Town tours depart four times daily from March to October (shorter hours November to February) from near the Florian Gate (p41). Look for a guide holding a yellow umbrella. Check the website for other tours. (📞 513 875 815; www.freewalkingtour.com; admission free; 🚊 2, 4, 14, 18, 20, 24, 44)

Cool Tour Company   CYCLING

12 👁 MAP P60, D5

Cool Tour Company offers a four-hour spin on wheels around town (90zł) that departs twice daily from May to September at 10am and 3pm. The tour takes in everything from the Old Town walls and Wawel Hill to Oskar Schindler's factory in Podgórze. Check the website for other cycling and walking tours. (📞 12 430 2034; www.krakowhiketour.com; ul Grodzka 2; 🚊 1, 6, 8, 13, 18)

Cracovia Walking Tours   WALKING

13 👁 MAP P60, D4

Two-hour walking tours, conducted by licensed guides, through the Old Town. Also does tours to Kazimierz and Podgórze. All tours depart from the Main Market Square (in front of the Adam Mickiewicz statue). Consult the website for a full list of tours and times. (📞 537 226 125; www.cracoviawalkingtours.com; Rynek Główny 1/3; admission free; ⏰ tours 10.15pm; 🚊 1, 6, 8, 13, 18)

Kraków Pub Crawl   WALKING

14 👁 MAP P60, D4

This tour, which visits four venues and includes unlimited drinks for an hour at the first bar, starts out from the Main Market Square, in front of the Adam Mickiewicz statue. Book in advance over the website or simply show up for the tour. (📞500 575 221; www.krawl throughkrakow.com; Rynek Główny; tours 60zł; ⏰9pm Mon-Sun; 🚃1, 6, 8, 13, 18)

Eating

Ed Red   STEAK $$$

15 🍴 MAP P60, D3

This is a solid splurge option for the steaks – cuts include New York strip, ribeye and T-bone – made from dry-aged beef and using only local producers. Other mains include beef cheeks served on buckwheat, wild boar and free-range chicken. The interior, with walls painted in muted blues and browns, is straight out of a magazine. (📞690 900 555; www.edred. pl; ul Sławkowska 3; mains 40-70zł;

⏰1pm-11pm Sun-Thu, to midnight Fri & Sat; 📞; 🚃2, 4, 14, 18, 20, 24, 44)

Cyrano de Bergerac   FRENCH $$$

16 🍴 MAP P60, E2

One of Kraków's top spots for fine dining, this restaurant serves authentic French cuisine in one of the most beautiful cellars in the city. Artwork and tapestries add to the romance and in warmer months there's seating in a covered courtyard. (📞12 411 7288; www.cyranode bergerac.pl; ul Sławkowska 26; mains 62-92zł; ⏰noon-11pm; 📞📶; 🚃2, 4, 14, 18, 20, 24, 44)

Wentzl   POLISH $$$

17 🍴 MAP P60, D5

This historic place, dating back to 1792, is perched above the Main

Chimera Salad Bar

ELENAPHOTOS / ALAMY STOCK PHOTO ©

Market Square, with timbered ceilings, oriental carpets and fine oil paintings all around. The food is sublime – cognac-flavoured foie gras, duck fillet glazed with honey, Baltic cod served with lentils and spinach – and the service is of a high standard. (📞 12 429 5299; www.restauracjawentzl.com.pl; Rynek Główny 19; mains 45-90zł; ⊗ 1-11pm; 🛜; 🚊 1, 6, 8, 13, 18)

Chimera Salad Bar VEGETARIAN $

18 ✖ MAP P60, C4

The ideal quick and simple Old Town lunch: grab a plate (big or small) and fill it with all those veggie items that look so good. The covered courtyard provides a delightful setting. Be careful not to wander into the restaurant of the same name downstairs, which is good but significantly more expensive. (📞 12 292 1212; www.chimera.com.pl; ul Św Anny 3; mains 15-30zł; ⊗ 9am-10pm; 🛜📶; 🚊 2, 8, 13, 18, 20)

Cakester BAKERY $

19 ✖ MAP P60, F4

Cheery throwback bakery with plenty of breakfasts, toasted sandwiches, pancakes and waffles on the menu, as well as excellent coffees and shakes. The big draw here is the attention to dietary preferences. Whether you're vegan, vegetarian or gluten-free, you'll have plenty of choice. (📞 12 307 0503; www.facebook.com/cakes

More Than Milk

Milk bars (*bar mleczny*) were designed as cheap, no-frills cafeterias, subsidised by the state during the communist era in order to provide simple meals for the poorest citizens.

Milkbar Tomasza (Map p60, F4; 📞 12 422 1706; ul Św Tomasza 24; mains 12-20zł; ⊗ 8am-8pm Tue-Sat, from 9am Sun; 🛜; 🚊 3, 10, 24, 52) is a modern take on the theme, where paninis sit proudly beside the pierogi.

Polskie Smaki (Map p60, D3; 📞 12 429 3869; www.polskie-smaki.pl; ul Św Tomasza 5; mains 12-22zł; ⊗ 9am-10pm; 📶; 🚊 2, 4, 14, 18, 20, 24, 44) borders on elegant, but the food is straightforward.

tercafekrakow; ul Św Tomasza 25; mains 15-30zł; ⊗ 9am-8pm; 🛜📶; 🚊 3, 10, 24, 52)

Cafe Botanica CAFE $$

20 ✖ MAP P60, C5

As the name suggests, the decor emphasises the horticultural. Breakfasts here are a popular choice. You can opt for a classic English breakfast, European breakfast, omelette or quiche. Pop in later in the day for a panini, burger or pasta, or simply a coffee and yummy dessert. Ample seating stretches way into the back,

with trees and plants aplenty.
(📞530 717 438;
ul Bracka 9; breakfasts 20-25zł, cakes
8-13zł; 🕙9am-11pm, to 11.45pm Fri &
Sat; 📶🍴; 🚋1, 6, 8, 13, 18)

Hawełka
POLISH $$

21 🍽 MAP P60, D3

Anyone who values art nouveau
or the paintings of Gustav Klimt
should be prepared to be dazzled.
Step inside and travel back 100
years. The traditional Polish food,
like Kraków-style duck, is nothing
to sneeze at either, and the daily
lunch specials (32zł) are excellent
value. Eat out on the main square
in nice weather. (📞12 422 0631;
www.hawelka.pl; Rynek Główny 34;
mains 48-64zł; 🕙noon-11pm; 📶; 🚋2,
4, 14, 18, 20, 24, 44)

Pimiento
ARGENTINE $$$

22 🍽 MAP P60, E6

This upmarket grill serves a diz-
zying array of steaks to suit both
appetite and budget, and offers
some reasonable vegetarian
alternatives for the meat-averse.
Factor the South American wine
list into your calculations, and you
have a classy night out. (📞12 422
6672; www.pimiento.pl; ul Stolarska
13; mains 40-130zł; 🕙noon-11pm; 📶;
🚋1, 6, 8, 13, 18)

U Babci Maliny
POLISH $

23 🍽 MAP P60, E2

This rustic basement is hidden
within the courtyard of the Polish
Academy of Learning. Simply
descend the stairs like you know
where you're going and follow
your nose to the dumplings, meat

The King of Pretzels 🍽

One of the unmistakable signs you've arrived in Kraków are the
stalls placed seemingly at every street corner selling the *obwarzanek* (ob-va-*zhan*-ek), a hefty pretzel. This street snack resembles
its German cousins, though it is somewhat larger and denser than
the average Germanic bread-based snack and is created by entwin-
ing two strands of dough before baking.

This popular ring of baked bread, traditionally encrusted with
poppy seeds, sesame seeds or salt, gives daily employment to myri-
ad men and women while ensuring them a dose of fresh outdoor air
(though selling it in winter must, admittedly, be less fun).

It's also a historic curiosity that has outlived numerous kings,
republics and military occupiers. There's evidence of *obwarzanki*
(pretzels) being baked as far back as the 14th century, and Cracovians still happily purchase them in large numbers as a quick bite on
the way to work or study – in fact 150,000 are baked every day.

dishes and salads. One of the specialities worth a try is the house *żurek* (a sour rye soup flavoured with sausage), served here in a bread bowl. (☎12 422 7601; www.kuchniaubabcimaliny.pl; ul Sławkowska 17; mains 12-25zł; ⏰11am-11pm Mon-Fri, from noon Sat & Sun; 📶; 🚋2, 4, 14, 18, 20, 24, 44)

Charlotte Chleb i Wino BAKERY $

24 MAP P60, C3

This is the Kraków branch of a popular Warsaw restaurant serving croissants, French breads, salads and sandwiches. The crowds on artsy Plac Szczepański are suitably stylish as they tuck into their croque monsieurs and sip from excellent but affordable French wines. The perfect stop for morning coffee. (☎600 807 880; www.bistrocharlotte.pl; Plac Szczepański 2; salads & sandwiches 15-30zł; ⏰7am-midnight Mon-Thu, to 1am Fri, 8am-1pm Sat, 8am-10pm Sun; 📶; 🚋2, 4, 14, 18, 20, 24, 44)

Europejska POLISH $$

Sure, the Polish food at this classic establishment (see 5 Map p60, D3) is good, but most people come here to soak up the old world atmosphere of the restaurant's back rooms. Striped wallpaper, green velvet banquettes and old gramophones lend a genuine 1920s, flapper-era feel. At the time of research, this place was undergoing renovation and let's hope they keep things just as they were. (☎12 429 3493; www.europejska.pl;

Rynek Główny 35; mains 50-60zł; ⏰8am-midnight; 📶; 🚋2, 4, 14, 18, 20, 24, 44)

Drinking

Bunkier Cafe CAFE

25 🚌 MAP P60, B3

The Bunkier is a wonderful cafe with an enormous glassed-in terrace tacked on to the **Bunkier Sztuki** (Gallery of Contemporary Art; www.bunkier.art.pl; adult/concession 12/6zł, free Tue; ⏰11am-7pm Tue-Sat; 🚋2, 8, 13, 18, 20), a cutting-edge gallery northwest of the Main Market Square. The garden space is heated in winter and always has a buzz. There is excellent coffee, unfiltered beers and homemade lemonades, plus light bites such as burgers and salads. Enter from the Planty. (☎12 431 0585; www.bunkiercafe.pl; Plac Szczepański 3a; ⏰9am-1am; 📶)

Café Camelot CAFE

26 🚌 MAP P60, E3

For coffee and cake, try this genteel haven attached to a theatre of the same name and hidden around an obscure street corner in the Old Town. Its cosy rooms are cluttered with lace-covered candlelit tables and a quirky collection of wooden figurines featuring spiritual or folkloric scenes. A great choice for breakfasts and brunches. (☎12 421 0123; www.lochcamelot.art.pl; ul Św Tomasza 17; ⏰9am-midnight; 📶; 🚋2, 4, 14, 18, 20, 24)

Lindo

GAY & LESBIAN

27  MAP P60, E2

A relative rarity for Kraków's Old Town: a gay-friendly bar and cafe within easy walking distance of the Main Market Square. The bar's located on two levels, with a big cellar that gets lively on weekend nights. The staff is friendly and welcoming. (✆798 648 143; www.facebook.com/LindoKrakow; ul Sławkowska 23; 🕑4pm-midnight Sun & Mon, to 2am Tue-Sat; 🛜; 🚊2, 4, 14, 18, 20, 24, 44)

Café Philo

CAFE

28  MAP P60, G4

Black-brick walls are lined with well-loved books and records. Worn leather furniture is populated by intellectual types who look like

they might be plotting a revolution. Chatty barstaff and clientele reassure you that they are not. (✆513 067 996; www.facebook.com/Philo Krakow; ul Św Tomasza 30; 🕑24hr; 🛜; 🚊3, 10, 24, 52)

Spokój

BAR

29  MAP P60, C5

Trendy young Kraków residents populate this hidden retro bar. Surrounded by colourful '70s-style decor, mismatched furniture and a permeating orange hue, you'll soon find yourself settling into the low sofas and being transported back through the decades. To find Spokój, go through the archway at Bracka 3 until you reach the end and walk up some steps. (✆501 652 478; www.facebook.com/spokoj cisza; ul Bracka 3-5; 🕑10am-3am,

Statue of Piotr Skrzynecki, Vis-à-vis cafe

noon-3am Sat & Sun; ; 🚋 1, 6, 8, 13, 18)

Pauza   BAR

30 🅿 MAP P60, E5

Walk up a flight stairs from within the **Pasaż Bielaka** (📞 535 519 602; www.facebook.com/PasazBielaka; ⏱ 4pm-2am Sun-Thu, to 5am Fri & Sat; 🛜) to find this beloved street-smart bar, known for its arty and alternative atmosphere. (📞 608 601 522; www.facebook.com/Klub Pauza; ul Stolarska 5; ⏱ 10-4am, to 2am Sun; 🛜; 🚋 1, 6, 8, 13, 18)

Feniks   CLUB

31 🅿 MAP P60, D4

Clubs in Kraków come and go with the season, but Feniks, hiding in plain sight on the main square, is still largely unchanged from communist days. The red-velvet curtains and white tablecloths lend a throwback feel to a time when couples still put on their best to rock around the clock. (📞 604 234 288; www.feniksklub.com; ul Św Jana 2; ⏱ 4pm-2am Tue & Wed, to 4am Thu, to 5am Fri & Sat; 🛜; 🚋 1, 6, 8, 13, 18)

Klub Społem   CLUB

32 🅿 MAP P60, D2

Just off Plac Szczepańska is this deceptively large underground bar and club. With communist throwback memorabilia covering the walls, and tunes of the '60s

through to the '90s, Społem is a cosy and fun find for a night of cheap beer and dancing. (📞 12 421 7979; www.pubspolem.pl; ul Św Tomasza 4; ⏱ 7pm-3am Sun-Tue, to 4am Wed & Thu, to 5am Fri & Sat; 🚋 2, 4, 14, 18, 20, 24, 44)

Vis-à-vis   BAR

33 🅿 MAP P60, C4

This cafe and stand-up bar is famous for having the cheapest beer prices on the main square and as a haunt of artists: painters, poets, singers and actors. The statue out front is of Piotr Skrzynecki (1930–97), the creative force behind the cabaret next door and a beloved regular back in the day. (📞 12 422 6961; www.zvis.pl; Rynek Główny 29; ⏱ 8am-11pm; 🚋 1, 6, 8, 13, 18)

Klub Pod Jaszczurami   CLUB

34 🅿 MAP P60, E5

This local legend student club has been going strong since the 1960s, and the black-and-white photos of performances down through the years that are plastered on the walls testify to its pedigree. These days, it's a mix of bar and dance club, with karaoke on weekends, and occasional live music and happenings. (📞 791 555 151; www.podjaszczurami.pl; Rynek Główny 8; ⏱ noon-1am, to 3am Thu-Sat; 🛜; 🚋 1, 6, 8, 13, 18)

Austrians & the Planty

The origins of Kraków's pretty **Planty Park** (Map p60, F1; 2, 4, 6, 8, 13, 14, 18, 19, 20, 24, 44) stem from a series of misfortunes going back to the partitions of Poland in the 18th century. In the decades after, Kraków was grabbed up by the Austrians, though no one knew what to expect.

The new administrators wanted to revamp the old Polish capital, making it less medieval-Slavic and more imperial-Habsburg. Decrepit dwellings, smelly stalls and charmless churches were torn down and brawny bridges and sanitising sewers were built up.

A main target of the reclamation project was the medieval wall. After five centuries, the barricade could no longer protect residents from modern artillery and siege tactics. The walls, towers and grandiose gates were dismantled, and the outer moats and trenches were filled in. In its place came a new green wall, a state-of-the-art park known as the Planty. Since the 1820s, the Planty has been the place to be in summer for seeking cool cover, with poplars overhead and lush lawns underfoot.

Entertainment

Harris Piano Jazz Bar
JAZZ

35 ⭐ MAP P60, C4

Lively jazz haunt housed in an atmospheric, intimate cellar right on the Main Market Square. Harris hosts jazz and blues bands most nights from around 9.30pm, but try to arrive at least an hour earlier to get a seat (or book by phone). Wednesday nights see weekly jam sessions (admission free). (☑12 421 5741; www.harris.krakow.pl; Rynek Główny 28; tickets 20-80zł; ⏲11am-2am; ☒1, 6, 8, 13, 18)

Piwnica Pod Baranami
LIVE MUSIC

36 ⭐ MAP P60, C4

This 'Cellar Under the Rams' has been a legendary place since it came into being in 1956 as a 'literary cabaret'. Nowadays, the program is a bit sporadic, but the space continues to host a summer jazz festival in July and several other concerts and cabaret shows throughout the year. (☑12 421 2500; www.piwnicapodbaranami. pl; Rynek Główny 27; tickets 20-30zł; ⏲11-2am; ☒1, 6, 8, 13, 18)

Stary Theatre

THEATRE

37 ⭐ MAP P60, C3

This is the city's best-known theatre company and it has attracted the cream of its actors. To overcome the language barrier, pick a Shakespeare play you know well from the repertoire, and take in the distinctive Polish interpretation. The box office is off Plac Szczepański. (Teatr Stary; ☑12 422 9080; www.stary.pl; ul Jagiellońska 1; adult/concession 70/40zł; ⏱box office 11am-7pm Mon-Sat, to 3.30pm Sun; ☐2, 4, 14, 18, 20, 24)

Teatr im Słowackiego

OPERA, THEATRE

38 ⭐ MAP P60, G2

This important theatre focuses on Polish classics and large-scale productions. It's in a large and opulent building (1893) that's patterned on the Paris Opera, and is northeast of the Main Market Square. Shows are often performed with English subtitles. (☑12 424 4528; www.slowacki.krakow.pl; Plac Św Ducha 1; tickets 30-70zł; ⏱box office 10am-7pm Mon-Sat; ☐2, 4, 14, 18, 20, 24, 44)

Jazz Club U Muniaka

JAZZ

39 ⭐ MAP P60, E4

Housed in a fine cellar, this is one of the best-known jazz outlets in Poland, the brainchild of saxophonist Janusz Muniak. There are concerts most nights from 9.30pm. (☑12 423 1205; www.jazzumuniaka.club; ul Floriańska 3; tickets 25-40zł; ⏱7pm-late; ☎; ☐2, 4, 14, 18, 20, 24, 44)

Jazz Club U Muniaka

Piano Rouge
JAZZ

40 ⭐ MAP P60, E4

This sumptuous cellar jazz club and restaurant is decked out with classic sofas, red velvets, louche lampshades and billowing lengths of colourful silk. Live jazz nightly around 9pm. (☎12 431 0333; www.thepianorouge.com.pl; Rynek Główny 46; ⏰9.30am-midnight; 🚊1, 6, 8, 13, 18)

Szpitalna 1
LIVE MUSIC

41 ⭐ MAP P60, F4

Awesome live music club and cocktail bar with an eclectic programme of electronica, rock and occasional stand-up comedy nights. The cocktail menu is equally eclectic, with lots of retro faves like Pina Coladas, Mai Tais, Brandy Alexanders and daiquiris. Check the club's Facebook page for a calendar and ticket prices. (☎12 430 6661; www.facebook.com/szpitalna1; ul Szpitalna 1; tickets 20-25zł; ⏰4pm-midnight Mon-Wed, to 3am Thu, to 7am Fri, 1pm-7am Sat, 1pm-1am Sun; 🚊2, 4, 14, 18, 20, 24, 44)

Shopping

Galeria Dyląg
ART

42 🔒 MAP P60, G4

This small, exclusive art gallery features modern Polish artists from the 1940s to the 1970s. Look for the Polish drip paintings, reminiscent of Jackson Pollock, from the late '50s. Many of the pieces on sale here are from artists now displayed in museums. (☎12 431 2521; www.dylag.pl; ul Św Tomasza 22; ⏰noon-6pm Mon-Fri; 🚊3, 10, 24, 52)

Galeria Plakatu
ART

43 🔒 MAP P60, E5

Poland has always excelled in the underrated art of making film posters and this amazing shop has the city's largest and best choice of posters, created by many of Poland's most prominent graphic artists. (☎12 421 2640; www.cracowpostergallery.com; ul Stolarska 8-10; ⏰noon-5pm Mon-Fri, 11am-2pm Sat; 🚊1, 6, 8, 13, 18)

Kacper Ryx
GIFTS & SOUVENIRS

44 🔒 MAP P60, F4

One-stop shopping for all your gift and souvenir needs. High-quality carved woodworking, pottery, traditional shirts and dresses - just about anything you can think of to stick in the suitcase to take home. Enter through the **Hipolit House** (Kamienica Hipolitów; ☎12 422 4219; www.muzeumkrakowa.pl; adult/concession 10/8zł, free Wed; ⏰10am-5.30pm Wed-Sun), a branch of the Kraków City History Museum that contains faithful re-creations of townhouse interiors from the 17th to early 19th centuries, which is situated next door. (☎12 426 4549; www.kacperryx.pl; Plac Mariacki 3; ⏰11am-7pm Mon-Fri, to 6pm Sat, noon-5pm Sun; 🚊1, 6, 8, 13, 18)

Piano Rouge

Salon Antyków Pasja   ANTIQUES

45 🔒 MAP P60, C4

This well-established antique salon is like a small museum; its three rooms are stuffed with clocks, maps, paintings, lamps, sculptures and furniture. Come to think of it, it's better than a museum, because if you see something you like, you can take it home. (☎12 429 1096; www.antykwariat-pasja.pl; ul Jagiellońska 9; ⏰11am-7pm Mon-Fri, 11am-4pm Sat; 🚊2, 4, 14, 18, 20, 24, 44)

Rubin   ANTIQUES

46 🔒 MAP P60, D3

Beautiful selection of antique jewellery, including many amber pieces, silver spoons, rings and watches. (☎12 422 9140; www.rubin.com.pl; ul Sławkowska 1; ⏰11am-5pm Mon-Fri; 🚊2, 4, 14, 18, 20, 24, 44)

Boruni   JEWELLERY

47 🔒 MAP P60, E3

One-stop shopping for amberphiles at this growing retail empire, with cases and cases of amber rings, necklaces, brooches and earrings, plus a 'museum' (free admission), where you can see how amber is cut, polished and set. Boruni includes a certificate of quality with each purchase. There's another branch and gallery (p49) at ul Grodzka 60. (☎601 824 646; www.ambermuseum.eu; ul Św Jana 4; ⏰9am-8pm; 🚊1, 6, 8, 13, 18)

Explore

Kazimierz

For much of its 700-year history, Kazimierz was an independent town with its own municipal charter and laws. Its mixed Jewish and Christian populations created a pair of distinctive communities side by side over the centuries. These days, Kazimierz does double-duty. It's home to many of the city's most important Jewish-heritage sites as well as its most popular cafes, clubs and restaurants.

The Short List

o *Galicia Jewish Museum (p78)* Pondering the fate of the region's Jewish population through photographs.

o *Old Synagogue (p86)* Learning Jewish rituals that were such an important part of life for centuries.

o *Remuh Cemetery (p86)* Glimpsing back 400 years to the origins of Jewish Kazimierz back to Renaissance times.

o *Temple Synagogue (p86)* Admiring the synagogue's lavish restoration that restored its mid-19th-century glamour.

o *Corpus Christi Church (p86)* Noting the size and prominence of this beautiful Gothic church.

Getting There & Around

🚋 Routes 3, 19 and 24 serve eastern Kazimierz, close to the former Jewish Ghetto.

🚋 Routes 6, 8, 10 and 13 run to the western part near Plac Wolnica.

Kazimierz Map on p84

Kazimierz cafe JAROSLAV MORAVCIK / SHUTTERSTOCK ©

Top Sight 📷
Galicia Jewish Museum

*This museum takes a different tack in exploring
Jewish history and the impact of the Holocaust.
Instead of presenting objects from the past, the
main exhibitions are built around hundreds of
contemporary photos of places that once played
an important role in Jewish culture and heritage.
The effect is to help us to see the past through the
present day.*

◎ MAP P84, H4

📞 12 421 6842

www.galiciajewish
museum.org

ul Dajwór 18

adult/concession 16/11zł

🕑 10am-6pm

🚊 3, 19, 24

'Traces of Memory'

The centrepiece of the museum is a moving photographic essay titled 'Traces of Memory: A Contemporary Look at the Jewish Past in Poland' that depicts modern-day remnants of the once-thriving Jewish community in the southeast of the country. The exhibition was the brainchild of the late photographer Chris Schwarz, together with Jonathan Webber.

'Unfinished Memory'

'An Unfinished Memory: Jewish Heritage and the Holocaust in Eastern Galicia', employs the same techniques used to explore Jewish history and memory, but pushes the geographic boundary to Eastern Galicia (today's Western Ukraine). Based on photos and text by Jason Francisco, the exhibit considers the continuing impact of Jewish heritage in the region.

Temporary Exhibitions

The museum has carved out a reputation for staging important temporary exhibitions that compliment the institution's purpose. Some of our favourite past shows include a series of video testimonies from Holocaust survivors and an exhibition on 'Polish Heroes: Those Who Rescued Jews'.

Cultural Programme

The museum goes beyond the writ of standard history museums by actively promoting and staging dramatic and musical performances. Many of these are timed to coincide with city festivals, such as the Festival of Jewish Culture, held in late June or early July. Consult the website for current events.

★ Top Tips

○ The museum also has one of the area's best bookshops, with plenty of titles on Polish and Galician history, Judaica and the Holocaust.

○ It also runs tours around Kazimierz and Podgórze as well as further afield to the Auschwitz-Birkenau Memorial & Museum.

○ This is one of the few important museums around town that is open on Mondays throughout the year.

✕ Take a Break

The museum has its own **cafe**.

Nearby **Bagelmama** (☏ 12 346 1646; www. bagelmama.com; ul Dajwór 10b; bagels 15-20zł; ⏰ 9am-5pm; 🛜 ✐; 🚌 3, 19, 24) has great bagel sandwiches and coffee for a quick pick-me-up. It also does light lunches, like wraps and bowls of chilli.

Walking Tour 🚶

Christian & Jewish Kazimierz

Most tours focus exclusively on Jewish Kazimierz, but the truth is that the district was home to important communities of both Christians and Jews over the centuries. This walking tour demonstrates that remarkable diversity.

Walk Facts

Start Pauline Church of SS Michael and Stanislaus

End Galicia Jewish Museum

Length 3km; two hours

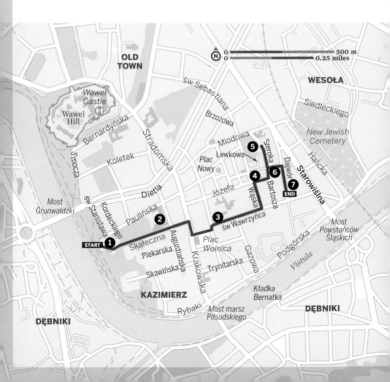

❶ Ancient Monastery

Start by taking in the impressive Pauline Church of SS Michael & Stanislaus (p89), with its mid-18th century baroque exterior (hiding a much longer history) and commanding views over the Vistula. The crypt below the main entrance holds the remains of eminent cultural figures, including Nobel prize-winning writer Czesław Miłosz (1911–2004).

❷ Gothic Splendour

Follow the tiny lane east to find the massive **St Catherine's Church** (Kościół św. Katarzyny; ☑12 430 6242; www.parafia-kazimierz.augustianie. pl; ul Augustiańska 7; ☉10am-4pm Mon-Fri, 11am-2pm Sat; ☐6, 8, 10, 13). This structure dates from the earliest days of the 14th century, when Kazimierz was a separate town from Kraków. The Gothic exterior is unchanged, and the spacious interior is used for concerts and festival events.

❸ The Parish Church

Cross busy ul Krakowska and Plac Wolnica to see another Gothic beauty, Corpus Christi Church (p86) from 1340. This was Kazimierz's main parish church. The stark exterior is Gothic, but the interior is baroque, with early-15th-century stained-glass windows.

❹ Entering the Jewish Quarter

Leave the historically Christian area as you walk east along ul Św Wawrzyńca and into the former Jewish quarter. Turn left at ul Wąska to see the evocative facade of the High Synagogue (p87). It's inactive today, but has an interesting photo exhibition on the second floor.

❺ Renaissance Cemetery

Wind your way east through the narrow streets until you end up at ul Szeroka, traditionally the centre of the Jewish quarter. Near the northern end are the 16th-century Remuh Synagogue (p88) and its adjacent cemetery.

❻ Sacral Objects

The late-15th-century Old Synagogue (p86) – true to its name – is the oldest surviving synagogue in the country. The museum inside is a great primer on local Jewish history and sacral objects.

❼ Moving Photography

Just outside the main Jewish quarter, along gritty ul Dajwor, the Galicia Jewish Museum (p78) aims to link the city's (and region's) lost Jewish heritage to the modern day through photographs and text.

Walking Tour 🚶

Gallery Hopping in Kazimierz

Kazimierz is great for hunting down quirky shops and galleries that go beyond the standard souvenir and amber shops. Rents are still low enough (though they're rising fast) to allow individual owners to hawk their own creations or to sell genuine antiques at junk-shop prices – though you'll need a good eye to distinguish the truly valuable from the merely interesting.

Walk Facts

Start Raven Gallery

End Błażko Jewellery Design

Length 3km; three hours

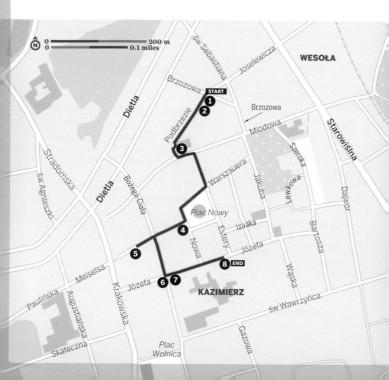

❶ Cubism to Modern

Art curator Zofia Kruk has assembled a small but impressive collection of Polish paintings from the 1930s to the present at her **Raven Gallery** (☏12 431 1129; www.raven.krakow.pl; ul Brzozowa 7; ☉11am-6pm Mon-Fri, to 3pm Sat; 🚊17, 22, 52). Prices are high but fair for the quality on offer.

❷ The 'Old Shop'

A tonic to the high-end art gallery next door. The very musty Stary Szklep (p99) toes that very fine line between antique shop and junk shop, and is fun to poke around in.

❸ Vintage Postcards

Galeria LueLue (☏728 551 024; www.luelue.pl; ul Miodowa 22; ☉11am-7pm; 🚊17, 22, 52) specialises in vintage photographs, including stunning black-and-whites of life in Kraków in the 1920s and '30s. Most are affordable copies, but there are some originals as well.

❹ Heaps of Memories

Descend into the cellar of the **Judaica Foundation** (☏12 430 6449; www.judaica.pl; ul Meiselsa 17; admission free; ☉10am-9pm, to 4pm Sat & Sun; 🚊6, 8, 10, 13) to find centuries of cast-off personal effects on display. Anything you can think of – paintings, posters, jewellery – you'll find in the piles down here.

❺ Retro Fashion

Vanilla (☏500 542 114; ul Meiselsa 7; ☉11am-7pm, to 4pm Sat, 10am-3pm Sun; 🚊6, 8, 10, 13) sells second-hand women's clothing from well-known international designers at a fraction of what the goods originally fetched in luxury boutiques.

❻ Contemporary Design

A self-described concept store, **Marka** (☏602 415 089; www.marka-conceptstore.pl; ul Józefa 5; ☉noon-6pm; 🚊6, 8, 10, 13) has a mission to promote the best Polish design in poster art, lighting, glassware, furniture and household items.

❼ Back to the Future

The communist period was unexpectedly fruitful in interior and product design. Poke your nose in at the **Szpeje** (☏798 504 458; www.szpeje.com; ul Józefa 9; ☉noon-7pm Thu-Sun; 🚊6, 8, 10, 13) branch in Kazimierz to see how fresh some of those old designs still look.

❽ High-End Jewellery

The eye-catching creations of Grzegorz Błażko are on display at **Błażko Jewellery Design** (☏579 056 456; www.blazko.pl; ul Józefa 11; ☉11am-7pm Mon-Fri, to 3pm Sat; 🚊6, 8, 10, 13), a small workshop n the heart of Kazimierz's gallery area on ul Józefa.

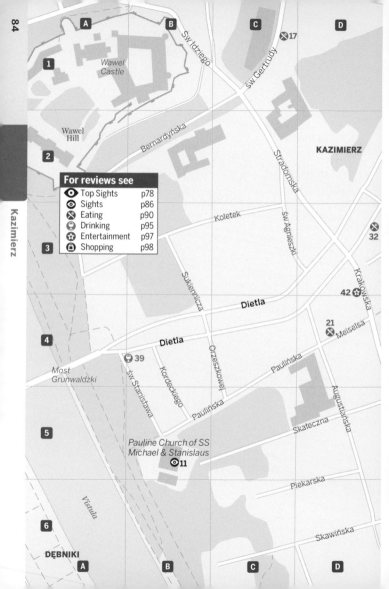

A   B   C   D

1   Wawel Castle

Św Idziego

⊗17   Św Gertrudy

Wawel Hill

2   Bernardyńska   KAZIMIERZ

Stradomska

For reviews see

⦿	Top Sights	p78
⦾	Sights	p86
⊗	Eating	p90
🍷	Drinking	p95
★	Entertainment	p97
🔒	Shopping	p98

Koletek

Św Agnieszki

⊗32

Krakowska

3   Sukiennicza

Dietla

⊗42

4   Dietla   Dietla   ⊗21   Meiselsa

Orzeszkowej

Most Grunwaldzki   ⦾39

Św Stanisława

Kordeckiego

Paulińska   Paulińska

Augustiańska

Skałeczna

5   Pauline Church of SS Michael & Stanislaus   ⦾11

Piekarska

Vistula

6   Skawińska

DĘBNIKI

A   B   C   D

Kazimierz

0 _____ 200 m
0 _____ 0.1 miles

Dietla

Dietla

48

Podbrzezie

Brzozowa

16

Miodowa

18 19 Jarden Tourist Agency

27

WESOŁA

Halicka

Rzeszowska

Dajwór

Starowiślna

38

4 Temple Synagogue

40

Kupa Synagogue

15

7

2 8 Remuh Synagogue

13

43

Miodowa

Bożego Ciała

25

37

Warszauera

Remuh Cemetery

20

Lewkowa

Szeroka

28

Plac Nowy Flea Market

5

Estery

Isaac Synagogue

9

Izaaka

Ciemna

High Synagogue

6

Old Synagogue

1

31

36

Plac Nowy

Meiselsa

34

47

35

22

Galicia Jewish Museum

Nowa

Józefa

26

Waska

Bartosza

Skwer Judah

14 Józefa

30

44

45

46

św. Wawrzyńca

Corpus Christi Church

3

10 Museum of Municipal Engineering

33

12 Plac Wolnica

Ethnographic Museum

24

Bocheńska

Gazowa

29

23

Bonifraterska

Mostowa

Podgórska

Krakowska

Trynitarska

41

Kładka Bernatka

Vistula

Sights

Old Synagogue MUSEUM

 1 MAP P84, G3

This synagogue, dating from the 15th century, is the oldest surviving Jewish house of worship in Poland. During WWII, it was plundered and partly destroyed by the Germans, but later restored. The prayer hall, complete with a reconstructed *bimah* (raised platform at the centre where the Torah is read) and the original *aron kodesh* (the niche in the eastern wall where Torah scrolls are kept), houses an exhibition of important liturgical objects. (Stara Synagoga; 12 422 0962; www.muzeumkrakowa. pl; ul Szeroka 24; adult/concession 11/9zł, free Mon; 10am-2pm Mon, 9am-5pm Tue-Sun; 3, 19, 24)

Remuh Cemetery CEMETERY

2 MAP P84, G2

This evocative cemetery stands just behind the Remuh Synagogue (p88) and dates to the Renaissance period of the 16th century. It was the quarter's main burial ground before it was closed for hygienic reasons in the late 18th century, when the larger New Jewish Cemetery (p129) was established. During WWII, the Germans vandalised the tombstones, but some 700 grave markers, including some outstanding Renaissance examples, have been recovered. The admission includes entry to the synagogue. (12 429 5735;

www.krakow.jewish.org.pl; ul Szeroka 40; adult/concession 10/5zł; 9am-6pm Mon-Thu; 3, 19, 24)

Corpus Christi Church CHURCH

3 MAP P84, F5

In the northeastern corner of Plac Wolnica and founded in 1340, this was the first church in Kazimierz and for a long time the town's parish church. Its interior has been almost totally fitted out with baroque furnishings, including the huge high altar, extraordinary massive carved stalls in the chancel and a boat-shaped pulpit. Note the surviving early-15th-century stained-glass window in the sanctuary and the crucifix hanging above the chancel. (Parafia Bożego Ciała w Krakowie; 12 430 5995; www.bozecialo.net; ul Bożego Ciała 26; 7am-7pm; 6, 8, 10, 13)

Temple Synagogue SYNAGOGUE

4 MAP P84, E2

One of the quarter's most visually arresting synagogues, the Temple dates from the mid-19th century. It was built in Moorish style and then given a lavish makeover in the past 20 years after being partially destroyed by the occupying Germany army in WWII. It's inactive these days, but still holds occasional concerts and special events. (Synagoga Tempel; 12 430 5411; www.krakow.jewish.org.pl; ul Miodowa 24; adult/student 10/5zł; 9am-3pm Mon-Fri; 3, 17, 19, 22, 24, 52)

Plac Nowy SQUARE

5 ⊙ MAP P84, F3

The centre of Kazimierz is marked by this popular square, with its signature early-20th-century roundhouse at the centre. This was once the commercial heart of the former Jewish quarter. These days it's a place to chill between bars and perhaps indulge in a *zapiekanka,* an open-faced sandwich consisting of a combination of baked cheeses and other toppings, sold from stalls in the roundhouse. Sunny days bring an impromptu flea market with vendors selling fruit, veg and discarded household items. (Plac Nowy; admission free; 🚋 6, 8, 10, 13)

High Synagogue SYNAGOGUE

6 ⊙ MAP P84, G3

This former place of worship was built around 1560, in Renaissance style, and is the third-oldest synagogue after the and Remuh (p88) synagogues. The High Synagogue takes its name from the fact that the prayer hall was situated on the 1st (upper) floor, while the ground floor was given over to shops. The synagogue is inactive and holds a permanent photographic exhibition on the families of Kazimierz. The ground floor holds a branch of the Jewish bookshop chain, Austeria (p99). (Synagoga Wysoka; 🖉 12 430 6889; www.krakow.jewish.org.pl; ul Józefa 38; adult/concession 12/9zł; ⏰ 9.30am-7pm; 🚋 3, 19, 24)

Plac Nowy

A Short History of Kazimierz

Though Kazimierz these days feels wholly integrated into Kraków, it wasn't always that way. For the first several centuries of its existence, beginning in the 14th century, Kazimierz was a separate town.

Jewish families started migrating here in larger numbers in the early 16th century, joining a growing and important Catholic population. Though the two religious groups were divided from each other, they co-existed (mostly peacefully) through the centuries.

The German occupation during WWII led to the destruction of the Jewish community here, and after the war Kazimierz fell into neglect and disrepair.

During communist rule, Kazimierz was largely a forgotten district of Kraków, and descended into something of a slum. Then in the early 1990s along came Steven Spielberg to shoot Schindler's List and everything changed overnight. In the past couple of decades, clubs and bars have returned to the area, bringing in a new permanent population of students and professionals.

Kupa Synagogue   SYNAGOGUE

7 MAP P84, F2

This small synagogue, which started life as a hospital, dates from the mid-16th century and was partly built into the Kazimierz city walls (still visible today). It was looted during WWII and only restored at the start of the 21st century. Notable features include rich ceiling frescoes from the 1920s and some unusual zodiac paintings. There's a small exhibition in the former women's gallery (upstairs) dedicated to Jewish life in Poland after WWII. (Synagoga Kupa; 12 429 5735; www.krakow. jewish.org.pl; ul Warszauera 8, enter from ul Miodowa 27; adult/student 6/3zł; 9.30am-6pm, to 4pm Fri; 3, 19, 24)

Remuh Synagogue   SYNAGOGUE

8 MAP P84, G2

Near the northern end of ul Szeroka is the district's smallest synagogue and one of only two in the area still used regularly for religious services. The Remuh Synagogue was established in 1558 by a rich merchant, Israel Isserles, and is associated with his son Rabbi Moses Isserles, a philosopher and scholar. The admission fee covers access to the adjacent cemetery. (12 429 5735; www.krakow.jewish.org.pl; ul Szeroka 40; adult/concession 10/5zł; 9am-6pm Sun-Thu; 3, 19, 24)

Isaac Synagogue   SYNAGOGUE

9 MAP P84, F3

Near the southwestern edge of the Remuh Cemetery is Kraków's largest synagogue, dated from 1638. Following partial destruction in WWII, it was returned to the Jewish community in 1989. Inside you can see the remains of the original stucco work and wall-painting. The synagogue has been restored and now houses a modest exhibition titled 'In Memory of Polish Jews'. There's also a small kosher food shop on the premises. (Synagoga Izaaka; ☑12 430 2222; www.krakow.jewish. org.pl; ul Jakuba 25, enter from ul Kupa 18; adult/concession 10/5zł; ⏰8.30am-6pm, to 2.30pm Fri; 🚊3, 19, 24)

Museum of Municipal Engineering   MUSEUM

10 ◉ MAP P84, G4

Trams and trucks fill the yard of this former tram depot, while inside there's a fun collection of cars and motorbikes. A room of hands-on magnetic and water experiments and some interactive science quizzes are sure to keep kids occupied, too. The museum is planning an extensive renovation, meaning that some rooms and exhibits may be closed on your visit. The museum is popular, especially on weekends, so book tickets in advance on the website. (Muzeum Inżynierii Miejskiej; ☑12 428 6600; www.mimk. com.pl; ul Św Wawrzyńca 15; adult/child 15/10zł, free Tue; ⏰9am-4pm Tue-Thu, to 6pm Fri, 10am-6pm Sat & Sun; 👪; 🚊3, 19, 24)

Pauline Church of SS Michael & Stanislaus   CHURCH

11 ◉ MAP P84, B5

Skałka, as this functioning monastery and religious shrine is called locally, dates to the early days of the Polish kingdom. In 1079, Bishop Stanisław Szczepanowski, later declared a Polish patron saint, was beheaded here by King Bolesław Śmiały (Boleslaus the Bold): the tree trunk where the deed was done is next to the altar. The church's baroque look comes from a mid-18th-century redesign. The crypt (closed December to February) shelters several eminent cultural figures, including Nobel-winning poet Czesław Miłosz (1911-2004). (Skałka; ☑12 619 0900; www. skalka.paulini.pl; ul Skałeczna 15; ⏰9am-7pm; 🚊6, 8, 10, 13)

Ethnographic Museum   MUSEUM

12 ◉ MAP P84, E5

The permanent exhibition here features the reconstructed interiors of traditional Polish peasant cottages and workshops, folk costumes, craft and trade exhibits, extraordinary nativity scenes, and folk and religious painting and woodcarving. The museum is housed within the former town hall of Kazimierz. It was built in the late 14th century and then significantly extended in the 16th century, during which it acquired its Renaissance appearance. (Muzeum Etnograficzne; ☑12 430 5575; www. etnomuzeum.eu; Plac Wolnica 1; adult/

Kazimierz Sights

concession 13/7zł, free Sun; ⏱11am-7pm Tue-Sun; 🚊6, 8, 10, 13)

Jarden Tourist Agency CULTURAL

13 ◎ MAP P84, G2

Mainly Jewish-themed tours, including two- and three-hour walking tours of Kraków's Kazimierz and Podgórze, as well as a popular two-hour driving tour of places made famous by the film *Schindler's List*. Tours are priced per person, ranging from 50zł to 100zł, depending on the number participating. (📞12 421 7166; www.jarden.pl; ul Szeroka 2; ⏱9am-6pm Mon-Fri, from 10am Sat & Sun; 🚊3, 19, 24)

Eating

Youmiko Sushi JAPANESE $$

14 🍴 MAP P84, E4

Tiny bar-and-table joint serving some of Kazimerz's best sushi in a casual, hipster-friendly setting. Lots of vegan items on the menu, and on Sundays it's vegan-only. (📞666 471 176; www.facebook.com/YoumikoSushi; ul Józefa 2; sushi sets 25-40zł; ⏱1.30-9pm Mon-Thu, to 10pm Fri & Sat, to 8pm Sun; 🛜🍴; 🚊6, 8, 10, 13)

Sąsiedzi POLISH $$

15 🍴 MAP P84, F2

A perfect combination of excellent Polish and international mains and unfussy, relaxed service. Dine downstairs in an evocative cellar, or in the secluded garden. The quality of the cooking rivals the best in this part of the city. If you've been hankering to try wild boar, goose leg confit or even horsemeat tenderloin, this is the place to give it a go. Reservations are recommended. (📞12 654 8353; www.sasiedzi.oberza.pl; ul Miodowa 25; mains 40-80zł; ⏱noon-10pm Mon-Thu, to 11pm Fri-Sun; 🛜; 🚊3, 19, 24)

Karakter POLISH $$

16 🍴 MAP P84, F2

Karakter feels unique in Kazimierz in that there's no theme or shtick, only a menu that promises a modern whole-animal, farm-to-table approach and unusual mains like horse sweetbread schnitzel and bull testicles. The sleek, understated interior puts the focus squarely on the plate. Service is excellent and the lunch menu (35zł) is a low-risk way of sampling the spoils. (📞795 818 123; www.facebook.com/karakter.restauracja; ul Brzozowa 17; mains 40-50zł; ⏱noon-11pm Tue-Sun, from 5pm Mon; 🛜; 🚊3, 19, 24)

Restauracja Pod Baranem POLISH $$

17 🍴 MAP P84, C1

Just what Kraków needed: a beautiful sit-down restaurant, complete with white linens and candles on the table and original art on the walls. It also just happens to serve gluten-free, well-done Polish mains like pierogi, potato pancakes and pork chops. (📞12 429 4022; www.podbaranem.com; ul Św Gertrudy 21; mains 40-70zł; ⏱noon-10pm; 🛜🍴; 🚊1, 6, 8, 10, 13, 18)

Polish 'Pizza' & Belgian Fries

Kraków has loads of restaurants, but come 11pm most serious food options close down. Thankfully, street-food purveyors keep going, giving you ample opportunity to quash the late-night munchies. Kazimierz, specifically **Plac Nowy**, is ground zero for 'Polish pizza' – otherwise known as *zapiekanka*. It's essentially half of a baguette, topped with cheese, ham and mushrooms. It's a cheap, filling snack that tastes especially delicious after midnight. Indeed, there may be no reason to eat it before midnight.

Not your cup of tea? No worries. Try out the various **food trucks** (Map p84, G4; www.facebook.com/skwerjudah; ul Św Wawrzyńca 16; mains 8-20zł; ⊙noon-11pm, to 1am Fri & Sat, to 10pm Sun; ⬛ 3, 19, 24) that have set up shop on an isolated square a couple blocks southeast of Plac Nowy. There you'll find burgers, ice cream, stuffed baked potatoes and a local favourite: Belgian fries. A more traditional option is to have a grilled sausage, served nightly (except Sunday) till 3am from a sidewalk vendor at **Unitarg Hala Targowa** in Eastern Kraków.

Dawno Temu Na Kazimierzu
JEWISH $$

18 ⊗ MAP P84, G2

Arguably the smallest and most atmospheric of several restaurants in Kazimierz playing on the old-time Jewish theme. The traditional Polish-Jewish cooking (think hearty variations of lamb and duck) is very good, and the warm, candlelit space, with klezmer music playing in the background, make this the perfect spot to enjoy this part of Kraków. (Once upon a Time in Kazimierz; ✆12 421 2117; www.dawnotemu.nakazimierzu.pl; ul Szeroka 1; mains 20-50zł; ⊙10am-10.30pm Mon-Sat, to 11pm Sun; ⬛ 3, 19, 24)

Hamsa
JEWISH $$

19 ⊗ MAP P84, G2

How can a place miss when it calls itself a 'hummus and happiness' restaurant? The light, uncluttered interior is a welcome tonic to the kitschy Jewish-themed restaurants in the area. The menu features a full range of Middle Eastern salads, plus spicy grilled chicken and fish. Good selection of vegetarian and gluten-free options. (✆515 150 145; www.hamsa.pl; ul Szeroka 2; mains 40-65zł; ⊙10am-10.30pm Mon-Fri, 9am-11pm Sat & Sun; ⬛ 3, 19, 24)

Szara Kazimierz
POLISH $$$

20 ⊗ MAP P84, G3

A step up in both price and quality from the several nearby

restaurants on ul Szeroka. Szara is the go-to if you're looking for dishes that are inspired by Kazimierz's Jewish heritage, like goose and rabbit, without being surrounded by klezmer music or Jewish-themed kitsch. Reserve on weekend evenings. (☏12 429 1219; www.szarakazimierz.pl; ul Szeroka 39; mains 60-80zł; ☻11am-11pm; ☎ 🖉; 🚋3, 19, 24)

Hummus Amamamusi

MIDDLE EASTERN $

21 🍴 MAP P84, D4

Hummus is undergoing a renaissance in Kraków and this tiny place on the western side of busy ul Krakowska has transformed the humble chickpea spread into an art form. Choose from various flavours, either 'classic' or seasoned with chilli, horseradish or garlic, and served in edible corn-flour bowls. (☏533 306 288; www.hummus-amamamusi.pl; ul Meiselsa 4; mains 20-35zł; ☻9am-8pm Mon-Fri, from 10am Sat & Sun; ☎ 🖉; 🚋6, 8, 10, 13, 18)

Massolit Cooks

VEGAN $

22 🍴 MAP P84, G3

Vegans and vegetarians will love this addition to the Jewish quarter. American-style bagels and desserts like pumpkin pie from the satellite bakery, as well as delicious veggie and vegan mains are on offer in this shabby-chic restaurant, part of a small local chain. Fans of Russian literature will also appreciate the origin of

the name. (☏12 422 1982; www.facebook.com/massolitcooks; ul Józefa 25; breakfasts 16-20zł, mains 18zł; ☻10am-5pm Tue-Fri, to 8pm Sat & Sun; ☎ 🖉; 🚋3, 19, 24)

Marchewka z Groszkiem

POLISH $

23 🍴 MAP P84, F5

Traditional Polish cooking, with hints of influence from neighbouring countries such as Ukraine, Hungary and Lithuania. Excellent potato pancakes and a delicious boiled beef with horseradish sauce are highlights of the menu. There are a few outside tables from which to admire the parade of people on one of Kazimierz's up-and-coming streets. (☏12 430 0795; www.marchewkazgroszkiem.pl; ul Mostowa 2; mains 15-35zł; ☻9am-10pm; ☎ 🖉; 🚋6, 8, 10, 13)

Good Lood

ICE CREAM $

24 🍴 MAP P84, F5

The Kazimierz branch of a highly popular ice-cream chain, featuring fresh, additive-free ice cream made from locally sourced ingredients. Order a cup or cone to take away. (www.goodlood.com; Plac Wolnica 11; per scoop 4zł; ☻11am-10pm; 🖉; 🚋6, 8, 10, 13)

Alchemia od Kuchni

BURGERS $

25 🍴 MAP P84, F3

Craft beers, burgers and hummus 'bowls' – a scoop of hummus topped with fish or beef sauce – all served up in a minimalist urban setting of exposed brick and concrete flooring. The vibe is just right for a casual meal and meet-up. (☏882 044 299; www.odkuchni.com; ul Estery 5; mains 25-30zł; ◷noon-11pm; �🖐; ☒3, 17, 19, 22, 24, 52)

Kuchnia i Wino MEDITERRANEAN $$

26 ✖ MAP P84, F4

The name, 'Cuisine and Wine', may not suggest lots of imagination, though the inspired Mediterranean menu surprises with lots of hand-made pastas and fresh seafood. It's hard to resist the garden setting, while the interior, with its sky-painted ceiling and Tuscan tones, is also inviting. (☏12 430 6710; www.facebook.com/kuchniaiwino; ul Józefa 13; mains 35-50zł; ◷12.30-10pm, to 11pm Thu-Sat; �🖐; ☒3, 19, 24)

Klezmer-Hois JEWISH $$

27 ✖ MAP P84, G2

Perhaps better than any other restaurant in the area, Klezmer-Hois evokes pre-war Kazimierz, with its tables covered in lace and artwork inspired by the *shtetl* (Jewish town). Warm up with a bowl of delicious soup invented by Yankiel the Innkeeper of Berdytchov. In the evenings, folks gather for concerts of traditional Jewish music (8pm). (☏12 411 1245; www.klezmer.pl; ul Szeroka 6; mains 35-60zł; ◷7am-9.30pm; �; ☒3,19, 24)

Ariel JEWISH $$

28 ✖ MAP P84, G3

One of several Jewish restaurants in and around ul Szeroka, this atmospheric joint is packed with

Kuchnia i Wino

old-fashioned timber furniture and portraits, and serves a range of traditional dishes such as goose neck stuffed with chicken livers. Try the Berdytchov soup (beef, honey and cinnamon) for a tasty starter. There's often live klezmer music here at night. (☎12 421 7920; www.ariel-krakow.pl; ul Szeroka 17/18; mains 30-60zł; ☉10am-midnight; 🛜; 🚋3, 19, 24)

Well Done BARBECUE $$

29 ❌ MAP P84, F5

Very likable barbecue and burger joint poised along shady ul Mostowa, with its string of trendy restaurants and cafes. The grillmasters know how to impart that smoky flavour to burgers, steaks and chicken breasts. The interior is kind of retro-diner, while there are a few picnic tables out front. (☎607 132 001; www.welldonego.pl; ul Mostowa 2; mains 25-40zł; ☉noon-11pm Mon-Fri, from 9am Sat & Sun; 🛜; 🚋6, 8, 10, 13)

Starka POLISH $$

30 ❌ MAP P84, E4

Starka is a fine dining experience you'll never forget. Meat lovers should try the pork knuckle, but only go full size if you've got a decent appetite. Starka makes its own vodka, so lovers of the drink are encouraged to be adventurous and try an unusual flavour. (☎12 430 6538; www.starka.com.pl; ul Józefa 14; mains 35-65zł; ☉noon-11pm, to midnight Fri & Sat; 🛜; 🚋6, 8, 10, 13)

Pierogi Mr Vincent POLISH $

31 ❌ MAP P84, E3

There are only a few scattered tables in this place, but there are about 40 kinds of dumplings on the menu – sweet and savoury, classic and creative. Maybe you thought you were tired of pierogi, but Vincent will convince you to eat one more plate! (☎506 806 304; www.facebook.com/pierogimrvincent; ul Bożego Ciała 12; mains 13-20zł; ☉11am-9pm, to 10pm Fri & Sat; 🛜🍴; 🚋6, 8, 10, 13)

Momo VEGETARIAN $

32 ❌ MAP P84, D3

Vegans and vegetarians will cross the doorstep of this restaurant with relief – the majority of the menu is completely animal-free. The space is decorated with Indian craft pieces, and serves up subcontinental soups, stuffed pancakes and rice dishes, plus a great range of cakes – some gluten-free. The *momo* (Tibetan dumplings; 15zł) are a treat worth ordering. (☎609 685 775; www.facebook.com/BarWegetarianskiMomo; ul Dietla 49; mains 13-20zł; ☉11am-8pm; 🍴; 🚋17, 22, 52)

Młynek Café VEGETARIAN $

33 ❌ MAP P84, E5

This vegetarian cafe is an ideal pit stop for animal-free soups and sandwiches, plus gluten-free traditional Polish mains like potato pancakes smothered in mushroom sauce. They also hold occasional

Pierogi

concerts, poetry readings and art exhibits. The terrace, overlooking the square, is a popular place to hang out in summer. (☏12 430 6202; www.facebook.com/cafemlynek; Plac Wolnica 7; mains 15-29zł; ☺8am-11pm; ☎🖉; 🚊6, 8, 10, 13)

Drinking

Hevre
CLUB

34 🍷 MAP P84, E3

After all of those tiny, cramped Kazimierz bars, spacious Hevre, occupying an enormous former Jewish prayer house, is a breath of fresh air. By day, Hevre serves as a civilised combo cafe/restaurant (mains from 25zł) and a superb place to chill over a good book or laptop. After dark, the crowds pile in for DJs and dancing upstairs

and downstairs. (☏509 413 626; www.facebook.com/hevrekazimierz; ul Meiselsa 18; ☺9am-midnight; ☎; 🚊6, 8, 10, 13)

Cheder
CAFE

Unlike most of the other Jewish-themed places in Kazimierz, this one (see **6** ◉ Map p84, G3) aims to entertain *and* educate. Named after a traditional Hebrew school, the cafe offers access to a decent library in Polish and English, regular readings and films, real Israeli coffee, brewed in a traditional Turkish copper pot with cinnamon and cardamom, and snacks such as homemade hummus. (☏515 732 226; www.cheder.pl; ul Józefa 36; ☺10am-10pm; ☎; 🚊3, 19, 24)

Pub Propaganda

Singer Café

BAR

35 MAP P84, F3

A laidback hang-out of the Kazimierz cognoscenti, this relaxed cafe-bar's moody candlelit interior is full of character. Alternatively, sit outside and converse over a sewing machine affixed to the table. (12 292 0622; ul Estery 20; 9am-4am; 3, 19, 24)

Mleczarnia

CAFE

36 MAP P84, E3

Wins the prize for best little beer garden – located across the street from the cafe. Shady trees and blooming roses make this place tops for a sunny-afternoon drink. If it's raining, the cafe itself is warm and cosy, with crowded bookshelves and portrait-covered walls. Interesting beverages available include mead, and cocoa with cherry vodka. Self service. (12 421 8532; www.mle.pl; ul Meiselsa 20; 10am-1am; 6, 8, 10, 13)

Alchemia

CAFE

37 MAP P84, F3

This landmark Kazimierz cafe set the district's shabby-cool aesthetic of candlelit tables and a companionable gloom years ago and is still going strong today. Alchemia hosts occasional live-music gigs and theatrical events through the week. (12 421 2200; www.alchemia.com.pl; ul Estery 5; 9am-2am Tue-Sun, from 10am Mon; 3, 19, 24)

La Habana   BAR

38 🚇 MAP P84, E2

Find a corner at this Cuban-themed bar known for its great cocktails and cosy atmosphere. Smokers can purchase cigars at the bar and enjoy them upstairs in the closed-off smoking area. Otherwise, grab a Cuba libre, chat to the friendly bar staff and settle into a low sofa to soak up the vibe. (Pub La Habana; 📞881 403 026; www.facebook.com/publahabana; ul Miodowa 22; 🕐10am-midnight Sun-Thu, to 2am Fri & Sat; 🛜; 🚋3, 19, 24)

T.E.A. Time Brew Pub   MICROBREWERY

39 🚇 MAP P84, B4

The first and only real-ale pub in Kraków was started by an Englishman with a taste for the proper stuff. Brewed on-site, the beer goes from cask to hand pump, producing favourites such as Black Prince and Misty Mountain Hop; the menu changes every week. Catch the weekly pub quiz on Mondays and settle in with some snacks. Pints 9zł to 12zł. (📞517 601 503; www.teatimebrewery.com; ul Dietla 1; 🕐4pm-1am Sun-Thu, to 2am Fri, noon-2am Sat; 🛜; 🚋Stradom)

Pub Propaganda   BAR

40 🚇 MAP P84, E2

This is another one of those places full of communist nostalgia, but so real are the banners and mementos here that we almost started singing *The Internationale*. Killer cocktails. (📞600 331 922; www.facebook.com/propapub; ul Miodowa 20; 🕐4pm-2am Sun-Thu, to 5am Fri & Sat; 🛜; 🚋3, 19, 24)

Cocon Music Club   GAY & LESBIAN

41 🚇 MAP P84, G6

One of a very few gay-friendly clubs in Kraków, this Kazimierz bar and dance club has two rooms, one with electronic music, the other more popular disco. Thursdays are given over to karaoke, while Fridays see a popular 'old disco' party. (📞503 773 844; www.klub-cocon.pl; ul Gazowa 21; 🕐9pm-3am Thu, 10pm-5am Fri & Sat; 🛜; 🚋6, 8, 10, 13)

Entertainment

Club Cabaret   CABARET

42 ⭐ MAP P84, D3

This red-velvet club harking back to the 1920s, both in appearance and programme, sponsors all types of shows from cabaret to burlesque, theatre, folk and just about anything else. Regular drag-queen revues are popular. Entry is down a dimly lit corridor off the

Jewish-Themed Events

In addition to the annual Jewish Culture Festival (p24) in late June and early July, the Judaica Foundation (p83) in Kazimierz maintains an active calendar of exhibitions and discussions.

Antiques & Flea Markets

Kazimierz is an excellent spot for antique and thrift shopping. While the Old Town is home to many of the city's more upscale places, Kazimierz specialises in scruffy junk shops where legitimate finds sit cheek by jowl with discarded junk.

The centre of the action, the **Plac Nowy Flea Market** (Map p84, F3; Plac Nowy; ⏰from 7am; 🚋6, 8, 10, 13), is best on Saturday and Sunday mornings, when it's crammed with stalls selling everything from clothing to comic books. On other days, you'll find scattered tables with fresh produce and antiques as well as Judaica and communism-related souvenirs.

street, but the mood brightens once you walk through the door. Check the website for details. (📞501 747 418; www.clubcabaret.pl; ul Krakowska 5; tickets 10-35zł; ⏰6pm-2am; 🚋6, 8, 10, 13, 17, 18, 22)

Oliwa Pub   LIVE MUSIC

43 ⭐ MAP P84, E3

This threadbare bar is one of the best venues in town for live rock and you'll find performances downstairs most weekends. Even if you don't happen to catch a show, relax over a beer and enjoy a stream of oldies from the 1960s and '70s over the speaker system. (📞608 125 081; www.facebook.com/oliwapub; ul Miodowa 14; tickets 20-30zł; ⏰10am-3am; 🛜; 🚋3, 19, 24)

Shopping

Paon Nonchalant   CLOTHING

44 🔒 MAP P84, F4

Be sure to peek in here at Paon, one of only a handful of women's clothing shops in town to focus exclusively on garments and accessories made by independent Polish designers. Lots of stylish bags, laptop cases and scarves at prices that just about everyone can afford. (📞534 484 399; www.facebook.com/paonnonchalant; ul Józefa 11; ⏰11am-6pm Mon-Sat; 🚋6, 8, 10, 13)

Austeria

EFESENKO / ALAMY STOCK PHOTO ©

Austeria
BOOKS

This evocative bookstore located on the ground floor of the High Synagogue (see 6 ⊙ Map p84, G3) has arguably the best collection of Jewish-themed books and Judaica, as well as themed-music CDs in Kraków. (✆12 430 6889; www.austeria.pl; ul Józefa 38; ⊘9am-7pm; ⊟3, 19, 24)

Lookarna Illustrations
ARTS

45 🔒 MAP P84, F4

Original hand-drawn postcards, posters, bookmarks, writing pads and magnets by artist Renia Loj that make for thoughtful gifts. Many of the black-and-white motifs evoke fairy tales and will appeal to younger kids. (www.facebook.com/Lookarna.Illustrations; ul Józefa 11; ⊘11am-6pm Mon-Sat; ♿; ⊟6, 8, 10, 13)

Asortyment Shop
CERAMICS

46 🔒 MAP P84, E4

This small gift and souvenir shop features handcrafted and other items made exclusively in Poland, including distinctive pottery and plates from the town of Bolesławiec. (✆608 833 513; www.asortyment.shop.pl; ul Bożego Ciała 22; ⊘noon-6pm Tue-Sat, 11am-3pm Sun; ⊟6, 8, 10, 13)

Antykwariat na Kazimierzu
ANTIQUES

47 🔒 MAP P84, E3

In the basement of the Judaica Foundation in Kazimierz, this Aladdin's cave is a jumble of antique china, glass, paintings, books and other assorted goodies. (✆12 292 6153; www.judaica.pl; ul Meiselsa 17; ⊘10am-5pm, to 2pm Sat & Sun; ⊟6, 8, 10, 13)

Stary Sklep
ANTIQUES

48 🔒 MAP P84, F2

Stary Sklep – the 'Old Shop' – toes that fine line between antique and junk shop. Indeed, you can expect to find just about anything here, from old rugs, dolls and clocks to retro postcards and evocative, tossed-away Judaica bric-a-brac that so sets the design tone in Kazimierz. (Old Shop; www.facebook.com/oldshopstarysklep; ul Brzozowa 7; ⊘noon-7pm; ⊟17, 22, 52)

Explore ◈
Podgórze

This working-class suburb across the river from Kazimierz would receive few visitors if it weren't for the notorious role it played during WWII. It was here the Germans herded 16,000 Jews into a ghetto before sending them off to concentration camps. The most important sights recall these events, including the famed factory of Oskar Schindler, where many lives were saved.

The Short List

○ **Schindler's Factory (p102)** *Experiencing the sights and sounds of life in Kraków during the German wartime occupation.*

○ **Pharmacy Under the Eagle (p107)** *Learning the story of heroic Polish gentile Tadeusz Pankiewicz, who helped the ghetto's Jewish residents.*

○ **Plac Bohaterów Getta (p107)** *Standing on the square where Jews first entered the sealed wartime ghetto in 1941.*

○ **Museum of Contemporary Art in Kraków (p108)** *Enjoying some of the best in Polish and international contemporary art.*

○ **Cricoteka (p108)** *Admiring the sounds and sights of the experimental theatre company, Cricot 2, and the troupe's groundbreaking leader, Tadeusz Kantor.*

Getting There & Around

🚋 Routes 3, 19 and 24 serve Plac Bohaterów Getta, the main jumping off spot for Schindler's Factory.

🚋 Routes 6, 8, 10 and 13 connect Podgórze to the western end of Kazimierz.

Podgórze Map on p106

Rynek Podgórski square (p105) with Church of St Joseph's
AGNES KANTARUK / SHUTTERSTOCK ©

Top Sight 📷
Schindler's Factory

An impressive interactive museum that covers the German occupation of Kraków during WWII. It's housed in the former enamel factory of Oskar Schindler, the Nazi industrialist who saved the lives of more than 1000 members of his Jewish labour force during the Holocaust – made famous in Steven Spielberg's 1993 film Schindler's List.

◉ MAP P106, F1

Fabryka Schindlera
ul Lipowa 4

adult/concession 24/18zł, free Mon

🕓10am-4pm Mon, 9am-8pm Tue-Sun

🚊3, 19, 24

Oskar Schindler's Office

For many years after WWII, Oskar Schindler's old factory lay abandoned. Thankfully, Schindler's former office survived intact. Here you'll see the names of the survivors and a symbolic Survivors' Ark made of thousands of enamel pots similar to the ones made by Schindler's employees during the war.

Documentary Film

A 30-minute introductory film features ordinary Kraków residents, including some of the former workers at the factory, who tell their own (often horrific) stories of life under German occupation.

Temporary Exhibitions

In addition to the permanent displays, the curators are committed to hosting thought-provoking and even controversial temporary shows within the overall theme of Kraków during WWII, such as a past exhibition: 'Liberation or Subjugation? On the Anniversary of the Battle for Kraków'.

Audiovisual Extravaganza

There's no one highlight here, rather the permanent exhibition is built around a series of rooms, each devoted to a specific theme, such as prewar Kraków, everyday life, the experience of Jewish residents, the resistance movement and the liberation of the city by the Soviet Union. Each theme is described with a mix of photos, radio broadcasts and video to create an immersive experience.

★ Top Tips

o Book tickets in advance online to avoid long queues at the ticket desk.

o Admission to the permanent exhibition is free on Mondays, but get an early start because the number of people allowed in is limited.

o On the first Monday of the month the museum closes two hours early (at 2pm).

o Note that the admission desk shuts 90 minutes before closing.

o A good-value family admission ticket is available for 55zł (for two adults and two children up to 16 years of age).

✕ Take a Break

Krako Slow Wines (p109), a little wine bar and restaurant, serves the best-value lunches near Schindler's Factory.

BAL (p113), located behind Schindler's Factory, has daily lunch specials and excellent coffee served throughout the day.

Walking Tour 🥾

Podgórze's Quirkier Side

Undoubtedly, Schindler's Factory and Plac Bohaterów Getta are the most visited attractions in Podgórze. But locals know this neighbourhood on the edge has more to offer, especially for travellers who wander off the beaten track. Wear shoes that can get muddy for this trek.

Walk Facts

Start Rynek Podgórski
End Płaszów Labour Camp
Length 5km; four hours

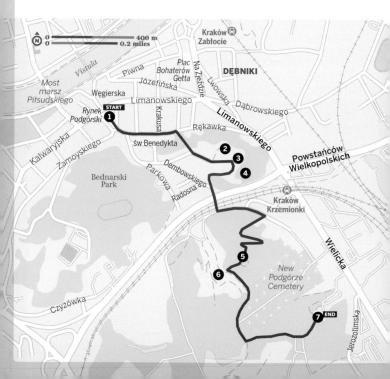

❶ Podgórze's Other Square

A world away from bleak Plac Bohaterów Getta, Podgórze's other square, **Rynek Podgórski** (🚋6, 8, 10, 11, 13, 19), is pleasant, green and integrated with the city. The square is dominated by the majestic Church of St Joseph, from 1905.

❷ Mysterious Church

Follow a footpath up to the ancient **Church of St Benedict** (Kościółek Św Benedykta; ul Rękawka, Lasota Hill; 🚋6, 8, 10, 11, 13, 19), one of the city's oldest and most mysterious churches. Archaeologists estimate it dates from the 12th century. The church is open once a year on the first Tuesday after Easter, when the festival of Rękawka is celebrated.

❸ Abandoned Fortress

Nearby, the abandoned **St Benedict's Fort** (ul Rękawka, Lasota Hill; 🚋6, 8, 10, 11, 13, 19) was built in the 1850s by the Austrians to defend the city from Russian or Prussian incursion. The interior is closed to visitors but you can still admire the two-story red-brick exterior.

❹ Forgotten Cemetery

To the south is the **Old Podgórze Cemetery** (Cmentarz Podgórski Stary; 📞12 656 1725; www.zck-krakow.pl; al Powstańców Śląskich 1; admission free; 🕐8am-6pm; 🚋6, 8, 10, 11, 13, 19), a burial ground that dates from the time when Podgórze was independent from the city of Kraków.

The cemetery was ripped up by the Germans during WWII and today retains a forgotten air.

❺ Pagan Mound

South of the cemetery, follow a footbridge across a highway to the prehistoric pagan site known as Krakus Mound (p108). Nobody knows the origins of the 16m mound, but legend says it may hold the remains of city founder Prince Krakus. Excavations in the 1930s uncovered artefacts dating to the 8th century.

❻ Creepy Quarry

Fans of the film *Schindler's List* will find the **Liban Quarry** (ul Za Torem, Podgórze; admission free; 🕐dawn-dusk; 🚋3, 6, 11, 13, 24) fascinating. Director Steven Spielberg used this overgrown, long-abandoned quarry as the set for the Płaszów Labour Camp – and indeed some of the old movie props are still standing.

❼ Forgotten Concentration Camp

Follow the footpath around the edge of the quarry and make your way to the remains of the real **Płaszów Labour Camp** (ul Jerozolimska, Płaszów; admission free; 🕐dawn-dusk; 🚋3, 6, 11, 13, 24). This forced-labour camp was built by Germans during WWII to facilitate the liquidation of the Podgórze ghetto. At its height in 1943–44, the camp held 25,000 people.

Podgórze

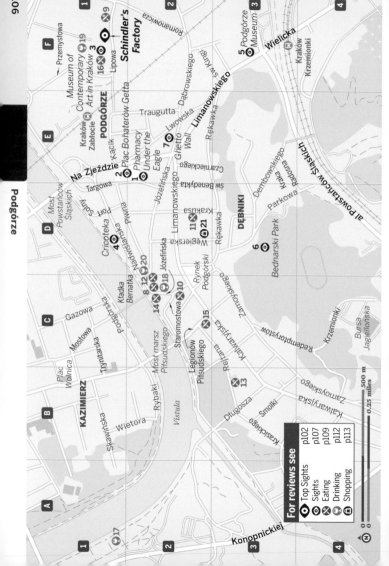

For reviews see

◉ Top Sights	p102
◉ Sights	p107
✕ Eating	p109
✕ Drinking	p112
◍ Shopping	p113

0 — 500 m
0 — 0.25 miles

Schindler's Factory

Museum of Contemporary Art in Kraków

Kraków Zabłocie

PODGÓRZE

Plac Bohaterów Getta

Pharmacy Under the Eagle

Na Zjeździe

Ghetto Wall

Podgórze Museum

Wieliczka

Kraków Krzemionki

DĘBNIKI

Bednarski Park

Rynek Podgórski

KAZIMIERZ

Cricoteka

Plac Wolnica

Vistula

Bursa Jagiellońska

Konopnickiej

Sights

Pharmacy Under the Eagle   MUSEUM

1 ◎ MAP P106, E2

This former pharmacy, on the south side of Plac Bohaterów Getta, tells the story of owner Tadeusz Pankiewicz, who risked life and limb trying to help the Jewish residents of the Podgórze ghetto during WWII. Pankiewicz, a Polish Gentile, was later honoured by Israel as being 'Righteous Among the Nations' for his efforts. The pharmacy's interior has been restored to its wartime appearance and tells the story of the ghetto and the role of the pharmacy in daily life. (Apteka Pod Orłem; ☏12 656 5625; www.muzeumkrakowa.pl;

Plac Bohaterów Getta 18; adult/concession 11/9zł, free Mon; ⊙10am-2pm Mon, 9am-5pm Tue-Sun; ⊜3, 19, 24)

Plac Bohaterów Getta   SQUARE

2 ◎ MAP P106, E1

Known as Plac Zgody during the German occupation of WWII, this public square marks the beginning of the purpose-built Jewish wartime ghetto that stretched for several blocks in this part of Podgórze (there is a map showing the extent of the ghetto on the northern edge near a former German command post). During the war, the space served as a meeting ground for ghetto residents. It was also a deportation site as the ghetto was liquidated in 1942–43. (Heroes of the Ghetto Square; Plac Bohaterów Getta; ⊜3, 19, 24)

Pharmacy Under the Eagle

Museum of Contemporary Art in Kraków
MUSEUM

3 ◉ MAP P106, F1

MOCAK is one of the city's most important venues for displaying contemporary art. The main draws here are high-quality rotating exhibitions, rather than an impressive permanent collection. As it's right next to Schindler's Factory, the two attractions can be combined for an absorbing day out. (MOCAK; ☏12 263 4000; www.mocak.pl; ul Lipowa 4; adult/concession 14/7zł, free Tue; ⏱11am-7pm Tue-Sun; 🚋3, 19, 24)

Cricoteka
MUSEUM

4 ◉ MAP P106, D1

This modern museum is dedicated to the life and work of avant-garde Polish dramaturge Tadeusz Kantor (1915–90) and his experimental theatre company, Cricot 2. Most of the exhibition is given over to the stage props and mannequins used in performances, the significance of which may be lost on non-Poles, but the space also houses happenings and theatre performances. Check the website. (☏12 442 7770; www.cricoteka.pl; ul Nadwiślańska 2; adult/concession 15/10zł, free Tue; ⏱11am-7pm Tue-Sun; 🚋3, 19, 24)

Podgórze Museum
MUSEUM

5 ◉ MAP P106, F3

More interesting than it looks at first glance, this museum tells the story of the district of Podgórze, which for centuries operated

as an independent town. The museum covers the history of the nearby **Krakus Mound** (Kopiec Krakusa; ul Maryewskiego, Podgórze; admission free; ⏱dawn-dusk; 🚋3, 6, 11, 13, 24) and runs through the time of the Austrian occupation all the way to the tragedy of WWII, when the area played host to many of the worst Nazi German atrocities. (☏12 426 5060; www.muzeumkrakowa.pl; ul Limanowskiego 51; adult/concession 12/9zł, free Tue; ⏱9.30am-5pm Tue-Sun; 🚋6, 8, 10, 11, 13, 19)

Bednarski Park
PARK

6 ◉ MAP P106, D3

Across the river in Podgórze, Bednarski Park may lack for picture-perfect quality but makes up for it with wild greenery fit for adventurous wanders. There are many levels to the park; you can clamber up walls and muddy tracks to explore paths hidden up high. It's a popular spot for dog walkers, joggers, walkers, families, and picnics or Sunday hang-outs when the weather is nice. Find the entrance along ul Parkowa. (Park Bednarskiego; Lasota Hill; 🚋6, 8, 10, 11, 13, 19)

Ghetto Wall
MONUMENT

7 ◉ MAP P106, E2

Just south of Plac Bohaterów Getta are the remains of the wartime Jewish ghetto wall from WWII, with a plaque marking the site. (ul Lwowska 25-29; 🚋3, 6, 11, 13 19, 24)

Podgórze's Heroes

Podgórze was home to at least two prominent Gentiles who risked their own lives to save Jewish people during the Holocaust.

The best known, of course, is Oskar Schindler, the heavy-drinking profiteer and antihero, whose story was told to millions through Thomas Keneally's book *Schindler's Ark* (1982) and Steven Spielberg's mega-hit film *Schindler's List* (1993).

Schindler originally saved the lives of Jews because he needed their cheap labour at his enamelware factory (p102), though he went on to use his connections and pay bribes to keep his employees from being shipped off to concentration camps.

The other was pharmacist Tadeusz Pankiewicz, who was allowed to operate the Pharmacy Under the Eagle (p107) in the ghetto until the final deportation. Pankiewicz dispensed medicines (often without charge), carried news from the outside world and even allowed use of the establishment as a safe house on occasion.

As is movingly quoted at the end of Spielberg's film, in reference to a passage in the Talmud, 'Whoever saves one life, saves the world entire.'

Eating

ZaKładka Food & Wine   BISTRO $$

8 ⊗ MAP P106, C2

This bistro specialises in simple French-inspired cooking centred on veal, rabbit, fresh fish and mussels, as well as several vegetarian items, and is one of the best places in the neighbourhood. Expect courteous but formal service and an excellent wine list. The simplicity of the presentation extends to the decor: beige walls, black tables and wooden floors. (☑12 442 7442; www.zakladkabistro.pl; ul Józefińska 2; mains 35-45zł; ◷1-9.45pm Mon-Thu, to 10.30pm Fri & Sat, noon-9pm Sun; ⋒⌨; ▣6, 8, 10, 11, 13, 19)

Krako Slow Wines   INTERNATIONAL $$

9 ⊗ MAP P106, F1

It's hard to accurately characterise this little wine bar and restaurant, which serves the best-value lunches within 100m of Schindler's Factory. The emphasis is on the wine, but it also serves excellent beer, coffee, salads, snacks and hummus sandwiches, and its Caucasian barbecue (Tuesday to Saturday) turns out mouthwatering Georgian- and Armenian-style shashlik and kebab. (☑669 225 222; www.krakoslowwines.pl; ul Lipowa 6f; mains 20-40zł; ◷10am-10pm Sun-Thu, to midnight Fri & Sat; ⋒⌨; ▣3, 19, 24)

A Dining Desert

Podgórze is something of a disappointment for eating. The area around Plac Bohaterów Getta and Schindler's Factory is a culinary desert, saved by just a few decent options. Elsewhere in the district, there's a clutch of nice restaurants at the point where the Bernatek Footbridge meets Podgórze (coming from Kazimierz), but don't stray too far from here as you're not likely to find very much.

Lody Si Gela · ICE CREAM $

10 · MAP P106, C2

Hugely popular ice-cream parlor, featuring all the usual hits plus lots of offbeat flavours like fiery wasabi. Vegans will find lots of options here as well. Line up at the counter and take away, though there's also a small eating area inside with children's books and toys. (☎609 475 537; www.sigela.pl; ul Staromostowa 1; per scoop 4zł; ☺11am-8pm; 🖊👶; 🚊6, 8, 10, 11, 13, 19)

Manzana · MEXICAN $$

11 · MAP P106, D2

Manzana is slightly more upscale than is usual for a Mexican restaurant in this part of the world, with a sleek interior and enormous bar. That said, the menu features the same mix of tacos, burritos and quesadillas you're used to, at reasonable prices for the quality. Creative mains like fiesta chicken pasta use tequila as a cooking ingredient. Reservations recommended. (☎514 786 813; www.manzanarestaurant.com; ul Krakusa 11; mains 28-36zł; ☺9am-10pm Mon-Sat, to 9pm Sun; 🛜🖊; 🚊6, 8, 10, 13)

TAO Teppanyaki & More · ASIAN $$

12 · MAP P106, C2

A bright, welcoming Asian restaurant, with a smattering of tables in a small garden out back – where there's also a children's play area. The emphasis is on Japanese cooking, with sushi, teriyaki and a selection of bento boxes. It also serves very good Thai food, with lots of vegan and vegetarian options to choose from. (☎725 880 304; www.taogarden.pl; ul Józefińska 4; mains 35-50zł; ☺noon-10pm, to 11pm Fri & Sat; 🛜🖊; 🚊6, 8, 10, 11, 13, 19)

With Fire & Sword · POLISH $$

13 · MAP P106, B3

Named after the historical novel by Henryk Sienkiewicz, this dark, atmospheric restaurant re-creates the Poland of yesteryear. The wood interior is made even more rustic with animal pelts and a roaring fire. The menu features well-researched old-time recipes, such as the succulent roasted pig that comes stuffed with fruit. (Ogniem i Mieczem; ☎12 656 2328; www.ogniemimieczem.pl; Plac Serkowskiego 7; mains 30-60zł; ☺noon-midnight, to 10pm Sun; 🚊8, 10, 11, 19)

Makaroniarnia ITALIAN $$

14 MAP P106, C2

Heaven for pasta lovers with a list of macaroni specialities as long as your arm. The cheerful interior makes for the ideal lunch spot, and the three-course lunch specials (20zł) are great value. Sit outside at one of the sidewalk tables in nice weather. (☎12 430 0147; www.makaroniarnia.com; ul Brodzińskiego 3; mains 25-35zł; ☺10am-10pm, to 11pm Fri & Sat; 🛜; 🚊6, 8, 10, 11, 13, 19)

Mazaya Falafel MIDDLE EASTERN $

15 MAP P106, C2

The Podgórze branch of a local chain of Middle Eastern fast-food outlets serves up excellent, life-affirming set menus of falafel and hummus. Most people order

to take away, though there are a few tables for dining in. (www.mazaya-falafel.pl; ul Legionów Józefa Piłsudskiego 2; set menus 14-20zł; ☺10am-10pm; 🚊6, 8, 10, 13)

Orzo ITALIAN $$

16 MAP P106, F1

This Italian combination restaurant/dance club is one of the few sit-down restaurants in the immediate vicinity of Schindler's Factory, though prices tend to be higher than the quality on offer and service can be indifferent. On the bright side: the eclectic menu of steaks, salads, pizza and pasta will appeal to all appetites. (☎12 257 1042; www.orzo.pl; ul Lipowa 4a; mains 35-50zł; ☺9am-midnight; 🛜; 🚊3, 19, 24)

Podgórze Eating

Polish fried pork cutlet

G8H007 / GETTY IMAGES ©

Drinking

Forum Przestrzenie
BAR

17   MAP P106, A1

In a highly creative re-use of an old communist-era eyesore, the Hotel Forum has been repurposed as a trendy, retro coffee and cocktail bar – and occasional venue for DJs, live music, film screenings and happenings. In warm weather, lounge chairs are spread out on a patio overlooking the river. (Hotel Forum; ☑515 424 724; www.forum przestrzenie.com; ul Maria Konopnickiej 28; ☉10am-midnight Sun-Thu, to 2am Fri & Sat; ☎; ☐8, 10, 11, 19)

Absurdalia Cafe
CAFE

18   MAP P106, C2

Arguably the most-welcoming of a string of similar cafes that runs along the first block you encounter just off the Bernatek Footbridge. Relax in an easy chair and enjoy the coffee and cakes. (www.facebook.com/absurdaliacafe; ul Brodzińskiego 6; ☉10am-10pm; ☎; ☐6, 8, 10, 11, 13, 19)

Story of the Podgórze Ghetto

At the outbreak of WWII and the German occupation, Kazimierz (not Podgórze) was home to most of Kraków's Jews. The area was closely integrated into city life, but at the same time retained its own feel, traditions and institutions. The German occupation, beginning in 1939, would destroy this centuries-old community within the span of little more than five years.

The first phase of the occupation was marked by severe legal limitations on Jewish life and forced expulsions into the hinterlands. In March 1941, the Germans initiated construction of a sealed ghetto in Podgórze. Later that month, around 16,000 remaining Jews were removed from their homes and forcibly moved across the bridge to the new ghetto.

By all accounts, conditions in the ghetto were abysmal. During 1942, new residents would be brought in periodically, while others would be mustered at today's Plac Bohaterów Getta and transported to the extermination camp at Bełżec, in the southeast of the country.

In March 1943, the ghetto was liquidated and surviving residents were relocated to a newly established forced-labour camp at nearby Płaszów, where many residents lost their lives due to unsanitary conditions. Most survivors were eventually sent off to extermination camps. Only around 3000 Kraków Jews survived the war.

BAL
CAFE

19 🚇 MAP P106, F1

Trendy industrial-style cafe and breakfast bar tucked into a repurposed warehouse in Podgórze's Zabłocie district. Great for coffee as well as light eats, sandwiches, vegetarian entrees and salads throughout the day. (📞734 411 733; www.facebook.com/balnazablociu; ul Ślusarska 9; ⏰8am-9pm; 📶; 🚋3, 19, 24)

Drukarnia
CLUB

20 🚇 MAP P106, D2

Not quite the legendary club it used to be, but nevertheless a reliable spot for a late-night drink and occasionally live music in the cavernous basement space. The ground-floor bar is divided into a scruffier half decorated to recall the bar's name (Drukarnia means Printing House), and a trendier but more sterile modern side. (📞12 656 6560; www.drukarniaclub.pl; ul Nadwiślańska 1; ⏰9am-1am Sun-Thu, to 3am Fri & Sat; 📶; 🚋6, 8, 10, 11, 13, 19)

Cawa
CAFE, WINE BAR

Chic wine bars like Cawa (see 20 🚇 Map p106, D2) are still a relative rarity in Podgórze. but here it is

complete with post-industrial decor and spiffy waitstaff. Come for cappuccino or cava. Also does sophisticated, Med-style tapas. (📞12 656 7456; www.cawacafe.pl; ul Nadwiślańska 1; ⏰8.30am-10pm, from 9:30am Sat & Sun; 📶; 🚋6, 8, 10, 11, 13, 19)

Punkt Docelowy
BAR

Chilled-out local boozer (see 10 ❌ Map p106, C2) just over the Bernatek Footbridge from Kazimierz . Good selection of beers and an ideal spot to start or end a pub crawl. (📞727 586 695; www.facebook.com/punktdocelowy; ul Staromostowa 1; ⏰4pm-1am, to 4am Fri, noon-4am Sat; 📶; 🚋6, 8, 10, 11, 13, 19)

Shopping

Starmach Gallery
ART

21 🔒 MAP P106, D2

Starmach is among the city's most prestigious galleries of contemporary painting and sculpture, exhibiting both emerging and established Polish artists. The striking modern gallery is housed in the former Jewish Zucher prayer house, a 19th-century neo-Gothic brick beauty. (📞12 656 4915; www.starmach.com.pl; ul Węgierska 5; ⏰11am-6pm Mon-Fri; 🚋6, 11, 13, 19)

Explore ◈
Western Kraków

Western Kraków is the prim and prosperous side of town, filled with tidy streets that are lined with well-maintained 19th- and early-20th-century townhouses. It's light on tourist attractions but arguably the city's greenest district. Thanks to the redevelopment of the former Tytano tobacco factory, now home to a motley crew of hipster bars, it's also one of the most popular party spots.

The Short List

○ **National Museum (p118)** Admiring the modern Polish painting on display or any number of temporary exhibitions on art or sculpture.

○ **Kościuszko Mound (p118)** Paying respects to the exploits of a Polish (and American) hero.

○ **Stained Glass Workshop & Museum (p118)** Touring a stained-glass workshop and learning about the skills that go into producing memorable pieces of stained glass.

○ **Jordan Park (p118)** Pondering the origins of this pretty park, which began life a century ago to promote the physical health of city residents.

○ **Józef Mehoffer House (p119)** Glimpsing the life of one the most influential artists of the 'Young Poland' artistic movement.

Getting There & Around

🚊 Routes 2, 4, 14, 18, 20, 24 and 44 service parts of the neighbourhood north of Old Town.

🚊 Route 20 is useful for reaching the National Museum and Jordan Park.

Western Kraków Map on p116

Kościuszko Mound (p118) DK-ART / SHUTTERSTOCK ©

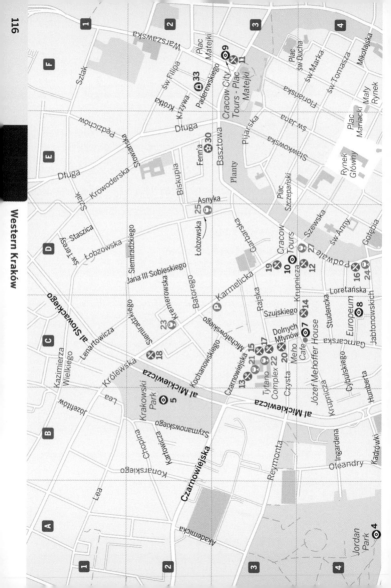

Western Kraków

For reviews see
- ⊙ Sights p118
- ⊗ Eating p121
- 🍷 Drinking p123
- ✪ Entertainment p124
- 🛍 Shopping p125

400 m
0.2 miles

Map labels:

Starowiślna
Westerplatte
Planty
św Gertrudy
Kazimierz
Dietla

Plac Wszystkich Świętych
Plac Dominikański
Old Town
Plac św Marii Magdaleny
św Idziego
Poselska
Straszewskiego
Planty
Wawel Castle
Bernardyńska
Wawel Hill
Podzamcze

28

Tratowska
Plac Na Groblach
Powiśle
Most Grunwaldzki

Smoleńsk
Stained Glass Workshop & Museum
Felicjanek
Retoryka
Wygoda
31
Mała
26
Zwierzyniecka

Vistula
Konopnickiej
Most Dębnicki

marsz Piłsudskiego
National Museum
3
Krasińskiego
Syrokomli
Włóczków
29
32
Ujejskiego
Dunin-Wąsowicza
Lelewela
Kościuszki

al 3 Maja
marsz Ferdinanda Focha
Kałuży
Filarecka
Krasewskiego
Prusa
Senatorska
Błonia Park
Fałata
Senatorska
Sławkowska

2
6

Sights

National Museum

MUSEUM

1 ⊙ MAP P116, B5

Three permanent exhibitions – the Gallery of 20th-Century Polish Painting, the Gallery of Decorative Art, and Polish Arms and National Colours – are housed in this main branch of the National Museum in Kraków, 500m west of the Old Town down ul Piłsudskiego. The most notable collection is the painting gallery, which houses an extensive collection of Polish painting (and some sculpture) covering the period from 1890 until the present day. (Muzeum Narodowe w Krakowie; ☑ 12 433 5744; www. mnk.pl; al 3 Maja 1; adult/concession 28/19zł, free Sun; ⊙ 9am-5pm Tue-Fri, 10am-6pm Sat, 10am-4pm Sun; ☒ 20)

Kościuszko Mound

MONUMENT

2 ⊙ MAP P116, A7

This mound, dedicated to Polish (and American) military hero Tadeusz Kościuszko (1746–1817), was erected between 1820 and 1823. It stands 34m high and includes soil from both the Polish and American battlefields where Kościuszko fought. The views over the city are spectacular. Admission includes the hike up the mound as well as a tour of the adjacent 19th-century fort, with exhibitions on Kościuszko's life. The memorial is located in Zwierzyniec, 3km west of the Old Town. (Kopiec Kościuszki; ☑ 12 425 1116; www.kopieckosciuszki. pl; al Waszyngtona 1, Zwierzyniec; adult/concession 14/10zł; ⊙ 9.30am-dusk; ☒ 100, 101)

Stained Glass Workshop & Museum

MUSEUM

3 ⊙ MAP P116, C5

This combination museum and workshop highlights the beauty of stained glass and the considerable skill (and artistic talent) it takes to produce it. Visits are by guided tour and tours in English are offered on the hour from noon until 5pm. (☑ 512 937 979; www. muzeumwitrazu.pl; al Krasińskiego 23; tours adult/concession 35/29zł; ⊙ 11.30am-6pm Tue-Fri; ☒ 20)

Jordan Park

PARK

4 ⊙ MAP P116, A4

Named after its founder Henryk Jordan, this park is a favourite for many. You'll find dog-walkers enjoying open fields, kids on climbing frames, outdoor yoga classes, and much more. Stretch out on the grass in summer, or try ice skating at the rink in winter. (Park Jordana; al 3 Maja 11; ☒ 20)

Krakowski Park

PARK

5 ⊙ MAP P116, C2

Renovated in spring 2018, this park is a lovely place to spend an hour with children, walking a dog or on your own. Added plants bring colour and attract bees to the area and you'll find ducks swimming in the central pond beneath a large overhanging willow tree. There's also a nook for borrowing and reading magazines and a fantastic play area for kids. (Park Krakowski; 🚼; 🚋 4, 8, 13, 14, 24, 44)

Zoological Gardens ZOO

6 📍 MAP P116, A7

The 20-hectare zoological gardens are well-tended and home to about 1500 animals. Highlights include a pair of Indian elephants, pygmy hippopotamuses, and a herd of rare Asian horses (Przewalski) that once roamed the Mongolian steppes. Bus 134 heads to the zoo from its terminus near the National Museum. (Ogród Zoologiczny; 📞 12 425 3551; www.zoo-krakow.pl; al Kasy Oszczędności Miasta Krakowa 14, Zwierzyniec; adult/concession 18/10zł; ⏰ 9am-5pm; 🚼; 🚌 134)

Józef Mehoffer House MUSEUM

7 📍 MAP P116, C4

The 'Young Poland' artist lived in this stately home from 1932 until his death in 1946. The museum preserves the elegant interiors, with many original furnishings and artwork. Look out for work by the artist, including stained-glass windows and portraits of his wife. Be sure not to miss the lovely garden. (Dom Józefa Mehoffera; 📞 12 433 5889; www.mnk.pl; ul Krupnicza 26; adult/concession 10/5zł, free Sun; ⏰ 10am-4pm Tue-Fri & Sun, to 6pm Sat; 🚋 2, 4, 8, 13, 14, 18, 20, 24)

Europeum MUSEUM

8 📍 MAP P116, C4

This oft-overlooked museum, housed in an old granary, holds

National Museum

Dr Jordan's 'Health Park'

These days, we take it for granted that parks and exercise go hand-in-hand, but it wasn't always this way. When Dr Henryk Jordan (1842–1907) first laid out what would later be called Jordan Park (p118) in the 19th century, parks were viewed as places to stroll and sit, but to work out? Not really.

Jordan was a pioneer for his time in physical education, particularly efforts to encourage children to get more exercise. Unlike other parks of its day, Jordan Park included football fields, exercise tracks and even a swimming pool. The kids were given free meals, provided, of course, that they got out there and earned them.

Today, while the park isn't expressly an exercise field, you can still see joggers making their rounds. Outdoor yoga classes and children's playgrounds complete the picture. In winter, an ice rink gives kids a chance to get a little fresh air. All of this would have made old Dr Jordan proud.

the National Museum's most important collection of European paintings. Around 100 works are on display, covering seven centuries of European art. Important paintings include Lorenzo Lotto's *Adoration of the Infant Jesus* (early 16th century) and a work by Pieter Brueghel the Younger. (Centre for European Culture; ☏12 433 5760; www.mnk.pl; Plac Sikorskiego 6; adult/concession 10/5zł, free Sun; ⏲9am-4pm Tue-Fri, 10am-6pm Sat, 10am-4pm Sun; ⛾4, 8, 13, 14, 24, 44)

Cracow City Tours - Plac Matejki

TOURS

9 ◉ MAP P116, F3

Runs a decent range of city walking and bus tours, including a popular four-hour bus tour, as well as longer day excursions to the Wieliczka Salt Mine (180zł) and the Auschwitz-Birkenau Memorial and Museum (155zł). Bus tours depart from in front of the office on Plac Matejki 2. (☏12 421 1333; www.cracowcitytours.pl; Plac Matejki 2; city tour adult/concession 120/100zł; ⏲8am-6pm; ⛾)

Cracow Tours

TOURS

10 ◉ MAP P116, D3

Offers walking tours of the city and a four-hour bus tour. English tours depart at 8.35am from ul Powiśle 7, which runs alongside the river to the northwest of Wawel Castle. Tour prices include admission. (☏12 430 0726; www.cracowtours.pl; ul Krupnicza 3; Kraków city tour 160zł; ⏲8am-4pm Mon-Fri; ⛾2, 4, 8, 13, 14, 18, 20, 24)

Eating

Glonojad
VEGETARIAN $

11 ✖ MAP P116, F3

This appealing and popular self-service cafeteria has a great view on to Plac Matejki, just north of the Barbican. The diverse menu has a variety of tempting vegetarian dishes including samosas, curries, potato pancakes, falafel, veggie lasagne and soups. The breakfast menu is served till noon. (☑12 346 1677; www.glonojad.com; Plac Matejki 2; mains 15-22zł; ⊙8am-10pm Mon-Fri, from 9am Sat & Sun; 🛜🍴; 🚋2, 4, 14, 18, 20, 24, 44)

Restauracja Pod Norenami
VEGETARIAN $$

12 ✖ MAP P116, D4

A warm and inviting Asian-fusion restaurant that's ideal for vegans and vegetarians. The menu runs from Japanese to Thai to Vietnamese, with lots of spicy noodle and rice dishes as well as vegetarian sushi. There's an inventive menu for kids as well, with items like dumplings with banana and chocolate. Book in advance. (☑661 219 289; www.podnorenami.pl; ul Krupnicza 6; mains 25-40zł; ⊙noon-10pm; 🛜🍴🚻; 🚋2, 4, 8, 13, 14, 18, 20, 24)

Międzymiastowa
INTERNATIONAL $$

13 ✖ MAP P116, C3

It's hard to classify this stylish, urban space deep within the Tytano tobacco factory complex. It's an excellent choice for a burger or casual bite, but many come simply to sip from some legendary gin-based cocktails, including those flavoured with rhubarb, peach, cucumber and thyme. (☑577 304 450; www.facebook.com/miedzymia stowakrakow; ul Dolnych Młynów 10; mains 35-50zł; ⊙9am-midnight Mon-Fri, from 10am Sat & Sun; 🍴; 🚋2, 4, 14, 18, 20, 24, 44)

Dynia
INTERNATIONAL $$

14 ✖ MAP P116, C4

While Dynia's interior is chic – with leather furniture and avant-garde floral arrangements – it is the courtyard that is the most enticing. Crumbling brick walls surround the fern-filled space, evoking an atmosphere of elegance amid decay. The name means pumpkin and there are plenty of pumpkin-based soups and mains plus other low-cal and vegetarian options – and a great selection of breakfasts (16zł to 25zł). (☑12 430 0838; www.dynia.krakow.pl; ul Krupnicza 20; mains 26-40zł; ⊙9am-11pm; 🛜; 🚋2, 4, 8, 13, 14, 18, 20, 24)

Veganic
VEGETARIAN $

15 ✖ MAP P116, C3

Veganic's cosy armchairs and outdoor courtyard make for a welcoming setting for very good vegan and vegetarian food, like tofu burgers, pastas and stuffed cabbage leaves. There's also lots of gluten-free items to try, and the staff goes out of their way to help you choose. Find it within the up-and-coming Tytano tobacco factory complex. (📞668 468 469; www.veganic.restaurant; ul Dolnych Młynów 10; mains 24-28zł; ⊗9am-10pm Tue-Sun, from noon Mon; 🛜📶; 🚌2, 4, 14, 18, 20, 24, 44)

Smakołyki

POLISH $

16 ❌ MAP P116, D4

If you like big portions and low prices, this restaurant just outside the Planty by Jagiellonian University is the place to go. Meaning 'treats' in Polish, Smakołyki is full of them. If not strictly traditional Polish food, it's nevertheless wholesome and delicious, and the view from the large window makes for great people-watching. (📞12 430 3099; www.smakolyki.eu; ul Straszewskiego 28; mains 12-30zł; ⊗8am-10pm Mon-Sat, from 9am Sun; 📶; 🚌4, 8, 13, 14, 24, 44)

Hanging out at 'Tytano'

A lot of the carousing in Kraków these days takes place west of the Old Town in a former tobacco factory just off ul Dolnych Młynów. The **Tytano** works lay abandoned for more than a decade before enterprising developers recognised the potential for an authentic hipster hang-out. These days, the six decrepit buildings of the old factory hold all manor of restaurants, bars and dance clubs, including one of the city's best vegetarian places and its premier craft-beer emporium.

Mr Pancake

AMERICAN $

17 ❌ MAP P116, C3

For decadent treats, this little retro number in the Tytano tobacco factory complex, is just the place. Stacks of American-style pancakes are covered with every imaginable ingredient, including Marshmallow Fluff, Hershey's syrup and Nutella. If you're into something savoury, check out the burgers – including a mac-and-cheese option. (📞664 091 109; www.facebook.com/mrpancakekrakow; ul Dolnych Młynów 10; mains 17-30zł; ⊗11am-10pm, to 11pm Fri, from 10am Sat & Sun; 🛜📶; 🚌4, 8, 13, 14, 24, 44)

Przystanek Burger

BURGERS $

18 ❌ MAP P116, C2

This is exactly what you need when you're in the mood for a quick and tasty bite, with appetising burgers that are every bit as good as the pictures. Choose from set options like Nachoburger and Bossburger, or build your own, including veggie versions. Seating is available upstairs, downstairs and outside. Located inside the Karmeland alcove. (📞661 577 751; www.facebook.com/przystanekburger karmelicka; ul Karmelicka 68a; burgers 13-22zł; ⊗11am-10pm, Sat & Sun noon-9pm; 📶; 🚌4, 8, 13, 14, 24, 44)

Trattoria Mamma Mia

ITALIAN $$

19 ❌ MAP P116, D3

We know you probably didn't come to Poland to eat pizza, but if you have a craving, go for the delicious,

crispy, thin-crusted variety that comes out of the wood-burning oven at Mamma Mia. Also serves good pasta, meat and fish dishes. (☎12 422 2868; www.mammamia.net.pl; ul Karmelicka 14; mains 28-56zł; �
noon-11pm; ☎🚾; 🚋2, 4, 14, 18, 20, 24, 44)

Bar Mleczny Górnik   POLISH $

20 ⊗ MAP P116, C3

A typical Polish milk bar, serving cheap, edible renditions of Polish classics. Turn up at the counter with a plastic tray, point to what you want and then try to find a free seat somewhere. The daily lunch specials (10zł) include a soup and main course and are excellent value. (☎12 632 6899; www.facebook.com/barmleczny.gornik; ul Czysta 1; mains 7-11zł; �
8am-6pm Mon-Fri, to 4pm Sat; 🚋2, 4, 14, 18, 20, 24, 44)

Drinking

Mercy Brown   COCKTAIL BAR

This hidden bar shows just how far word-of-mouth goes (see 16 ⊗ Map p116, D4). It's not easy to find – nevertheless, it's so popular you need a reservation to get in. The allure is obvious: a taste of the 1920s, with low-lit chandeliers, plush armchairs and a long bar stacked with liquor. Monthly burlesque shows, jazz concerts and artistically made cocktails make this a unique experience. (☎531 706 692; ul Straszewskiego 28; �
7pm-1.30am Wed & Thu, to 2.30am Fri & Sat; ☎; 🚋4, 8, 13, 14, 24, 44)

Weźże Krafta   CRAFT BEER

21 🚇 MAP P116, C3

Just what Kraków needed: a warehouse-sized craft beer emporium with something like 25 craft beers on tap and enough space to handle loud, rowdy groups. It's situated toward the middle of the popular Tytano complex. It's understandably popular, meaning your best plan is to arrive early to grab a table. (☎12 307 4050; www.wezze-krafta.ontap.pl; ul Dolnych Młynów 10; �
4pm-2am Mon-Fri, from 2pm Sat & Sun; ☎; 🚋2, 4, 14, 18, 20, 24, 44)

Scena54   CLUB

22 🚇 MAP P116, C3

The name harkens back to bawdy New York of the 1980s, and the Scena54 dance club is aimed at older guests (here meaning 30s to 50s), who might still have hazy memories of those days. Check the website for special throwback, DJ and ladies' nights that are sure to bring out the crowds. The club is located in the Tytano complex. (☎12 378 3778; www.scena54.pl; ul Dolnych Młynów 10; ☎
7pm-1am Wed & Thu, to 4am Fri & Sat; ☎; 🚋2, 4, 14, 18, 20, 24, 44)

Piwiarnia Warka   PUB

23 🚇 MAP P116, C2

This informal pub/restaurant perches on one of the busiest streets in Kraków, but its outdoor annex is sheltered enough to provide an ideal combination of privacy and people-watching. It's an especially popular place during football (soccer) matches. The beer bites, pizzas and burgers (23zł to 28zł) are decent, too, and reasonably priced. (☎508 318 115; www.facebook.com/PiwiarniaKrakow; ul Karmelicka 43a; ☺noon-midnight; ☎; 🚊4, 8, 13, 14, 24, 44)

Stary Port PUB

24 🚇 MAP P116, D4

Old Port is a roomy, rummy pub with a distinct nautical theme, with maps, flags and ship-related kitsch adorning the walls. With some of the cheapest drinks this close to the centre and live music on Fridays, it's deservedly popular. Enter from ul Jabłonowskich. (☎508 227 752; www.staryport.com.pl; ul Straszewskiego 27; ☺noon-midnight, to 3am Fri & Sat; ☎; 🚊1, 6, 8, 13, 18)

The Stage BAR

25 🚇 MAP P116, D2

This combo sports bar and billiards hall, situated a few minutes' walk from the centre, is a great place to chill out. If you're looking to shoot a game of pool, it's best to book in advance. If not, simply enjoy the atmosphere over drinks and maybe catch a sporting event on the TV. (☎12 681 6385; www.facebook.com/thestagee; ul Łobzowska 3; ☺noon-1am; ☎; 🚊2, 4, 14, 18, 20, 24, 44)

Café Szafe CAFE

26 🚇 MAP P116, C6

The colourful cafe on the corner is a cupboard full of surprises, from the whimsical sculptured creatures lurking in the corners to the intriguing artwork that hangs on the walls. The place hosts concerts, films and other arty events. (☎663 905 652; www.cafeszafe.com; ul Felicjanek 10; ☺9am-2am Mon-Fri, from 10am Sat & Sun; ☎; 🚊1, 2, 6)

CK Browar MICROBREWERY

27 🚇 MAP P116, D4

Serious tipplers will head for this below-ground microbrewery with its cavernous drinking hall. The amber fluid is brewed on the spot to an old Austro-Hungarian recipe, then poured straight from the tanks into patrons' glasses. Beware the CK Dunkel brew, which is about 7% alcohol. (☎12 429 2505; www.ckbrowar.krakow.pl; ul Podwale 6/7; ☺9am-1am; ☎; 🚊2, 4, 11, 18, 20, 24, 44)

Entertainment

Kraków Philharmonic CLASSICAL MUSIC

28 ⭐ MAP P116, D5

Home to one of Poland's best orchestras. Check the website for a calendar of events. Buy tickets at the box office during working hours or an hour ahead of the performance. (Filharmonia im Karola Szymanowskiego w Krakowie; ☎12 619 8733; www.filharmonia.krakow.pl; ul Zwierzyniecka 1; 🚊1, 2, 6)

Kino Kijów Centrum CINEMA

29 ⭐ MAP P116, B5

Loved by Cracovians for its retro '60s, communist-era design and architecture, Kijów is one of many independent cinemas in

Kraków. It's also home to a film cafe (open from 10am to 10pm) and club featuring live performances. There are several small and medium-sized cinemas, with 20 to 40 seats, and a larger hall that accommodates more than 800 – the largest screening room in Kraków. (☑12 433 0033; www.kijow.pl; al Krasińskiego 34; tickets 16-20zł; ☐20)

Florianka Recital Hall

CLASSICAL MUSIC

30 ⭐ MAP P116, E2

The recital hall of the Kraków Academy of Music. Check the website for upcoming chamber concerts. Also hosts the annual **Bach Days music festival** (Dni Bachowskie; www.bach-cantatas.com; ☺mid-Mar). (Aula Florianka; ☑12 422 5173; www.amuz.krakow.pl; ul Sereno Fenn'a 15)

Shopping

Massolit Books & Cafe

BOOKS

31 🅐 MAP P116, C5

Highly atmospheric book emporium selling English-language fiction and nonfiction, both new and secondhand. There's a cafe area with loads of character, starting among the bookshelves and extending into a moody back room. The collection is particularly strong on Polish and Central European authors in translation. (☑12 432 4150; www.massolit.com; ul Felicjanek 4; ☺10am-8pm Sun-Thu, to 9pm Fri & Sat; ☎; ☐1, 2, 6)

A Hidden Garden

The secluded garden behind the **Meho Cafe** (Map p116, C4; ☑600 480 049; www.facebook.com/MehoCafe; ul Krupnicza 26; ☺10am-10pm; ☎; ☐2, 4, 8, 13, 14, 18, 20, 24) is a little piece of paradise in the middle of the city and the perfect spot for a cooling beverage on a hot day.

Dydo Poster Gallery

ART

32 🅐 MAP P116, B5

Poles are recognised around the world for the quality and artistry of their poster art. You'll find some of the best historic and retro posters as well as more modern designs here. (Dydo Galeria Plakatu; ☑790 792 244; www.dydopostergallery.com; al Focha 1; ☺2.30-6.30pm; ☐20)

Stary Kleparz

MARKET

33 🅐 MAP P116, F2

The city's most atmospheric and historic place to shop for fresh fruits, vegetables and flowers is this sprawling covered market, which dates back to the 12th century. You'll also find meats, cheeses, spices and bread, as well as clothes and other necessities. (☑12 634 1532; www.starykleparz.com; ul Paderewskiego, Rynek Kleparski; ☺6am-6pm Mon-Fri, to 4pm Sat, 8am-3pm Sun; ☐2, 4, 14, 18, 20, 24, 44)

POD
TWOJĄ OBRONĘ
UCIEKAMY SIĘ.

GROB RODZIN

Explore ◈
Eastern Kraków

Most visitors to Kraków arrive at the train or bus stations in the eastern part of the city and then beat a hasty path into the Old Town. Yet, Eastern Kraków is where the city pulses to a different beat. Here, Kraków loses its aura of medieval magic and holiday haven and takes on the rhythms of the workaday world.

The Short List

◦ **New Jewish Cemetery (p129)** *Staring in amazement at the sheer number of graves and the resolve of survivors to remember the dead.*

◦ **Rakowicki Cemetery (p130)** *Gawking at the artistry of the headstones, from multi-tiered neo-Gothic to daring art nouveau examples.*

◦ **Botanical Gardens (p130)** *Admiring the many hectares of green and flowery loveliness.*

◦ **History Land (p130)** *Focusing on Polish history while being bombarded by high-tech sounds and sensations.*

◦ **Opera Krakowska (p133)** *Adding a highbrow musical dimension to your explorations.*

Getting There & Around

🚌 Routes 2, 3, 4, 5, 10, 14, 17, 19, 20, 44, 50, 52 serve the main train station and bus stations.

🚌 Routes 3, 19, 24 run further south toward the Galeria Kazimierz.

Eastern Kraków Map on p128

Rakowicki Cemetery (p130) AGNES KANTARUK / SHUTTERSTOCK ©

For reviews see

◉	Sights	p129
✕	Eating	p131
🍺	Drinking	p132
★	Entertainment	p133
🛍	Shopping	p133

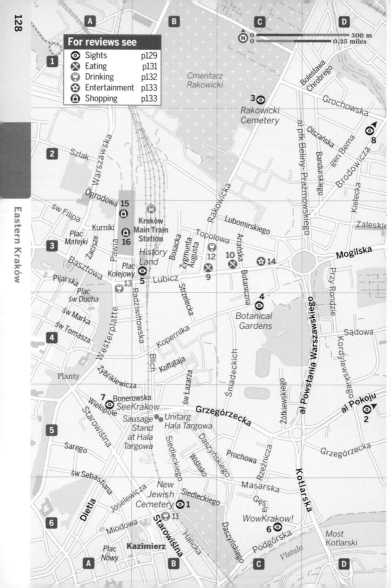

500 m
0.25 miles

Cmentarz Rakowicki

Rakowicki Cemetery 3

8

Szlak

Warszawska

Ogrodowa

św Filipa

Kurniki

Plac Matejki

Zacisze

Pawia

Basztowa

Radziwiłłowska

Pijarska

Plac św Ducha

św Marka

św Tomasza

Planty

Westerplatte

Blich

Kopernika

Kołłątaja

Żyblikiewicza

Bonerowska

Wielopole

SeeKraków

Starowiślna

Dietla

Joselewicza

Sarego

św Sebastiana

Kraków Main Train Station

History Land

Plac Kolejowy

15

16

13

5

Lubicz

Bosacka

Strzelecka

św Łazarza

Zamenhofa

Siedleckiego

Wiślisko

New Jewish Cemetery 1

Miodowa

Plac Nowy

Kazimierz

Halicka

Grochowska

Bolesława Chrobrego

Olszańska

al płk Beliny-Prażmowskiego

gen Bema

Bandurskiego

Brodowicza

Kielecka

Zaleskie

Lubomirskiego

Rakowicka

Topolowa

Zygmunta Augusta

Ariańska

Botaniczna

12

10

14

9

4

Botanical Gardens

Śniadeckich

Grzegórzecka

Żółkiewskiego

al Powstania Warszawskiego

Mogilska

Przy Rondzie

Sądowa

Kordylewskiego

al Pokoju

2

Grzegórzecka

Kotlarska

Unitarg Hala Targowa

Sausage Stand at Hala Targowa

Daszyńskiego

Prochowa

Rzeźnicza

Gęsi

Masarska

Podgórska

WowKraków! 6

11

Most Kotlarski

Vistula

Zaleskie

Sights

New Jewish Cemetery CEMETERY

1 ⊙ MAP P128, B6

This enormous cemetery dates from 1800 and was the main burial ground for Kazimierz's Jewish population up until WWII. Many of the grave markers were destroyed during the German occupation and some of the recovered tombstones are visible on the cemetery walls. Around 9000 tombstones are still visible, though many remain untended as whole families perished in the Holocaust. Follow ul Miodowa below a railway bridge and find the small gate to the cemetery. (Nowy Cmentarz Żidowsky; ul Miodowa 55; ☉9am-6pm Sun-Thu; 🚋3, 19, 24)

Stanisław Lem Science Garden MUSEUM

2 ⊙ MAP P128, D5

Science nerds will enjoy a day out at this interactive science park, about 4km east of the Old Town, dedicated to the memory of Polish science fiction writer Stanisław Lem. The outdoor exhibits explore some of the bizarre consequences of the laws of science, mechanics, optics and acoustics, and invite visitors to get involved, peering through prisms and striking gongs. Explanations are in both Polish and English. (📞12 346 1285; www. ogroddoswiadczen.pl; al Pokoju 68, Czyżyny; adult/concession 12/10zł; ☉8.30am-7pm Mon-Fri, from 10am Sat & Sun Apr-Sep, shorter hours Oct; 👪; 🚋1, 14, 22)

New Jewish Cemetery

KDN759 / SHUTTERSTOCK ©

Paying Respects at the New Jewish Cemetery

Strolling through Kraków's lively streets, the Holocaust and the tragedy of WWII for the Jewish people can feel far away. This forgotten cemetery (p129), located in a remote part of Eastern Kraków beyond a train underpass, retains something of the sadness of those days. The Nazis made short work of the cemetery during the war and used many of the grave markers as paving stones and scrap. It's touching to see how much effort has gone into trying to restore the cemetery and rescue the remnants that could be recovered.

Rakowicki Cemetery CEMETERY

3 MAP P128, C1

Arguably the city's most prestigious burial ground and the final resting place of several notable Poles, including Wisława Szymborska (1923–2012), the 1996 Nobel prize winner for literature. Stroll through the grounds to admire the beautifully crafted tombstones, many of which are works of art in their own right. (Cmentarz Rakowicki; ☑12 619 9900; www.zck-krakow.pl; ul Rakowicka 26; ☉7am-6pm; 🚃2)

Botanical Gardens GARDENS

4 ⦿ MAP P128, C4

The botanical gardens of Jagiellonian University comprise nearly ten hectares of green and flowery loveliness. Besides the fresh air and beautiful blooms, the gardens offer fascinating exhibits of medicinal plants, endangered species of Polish flora, and plants described in the Bible. The amazing orchid collection dates to the 1860s. (Ogród Botaniczny; ☑12 663 3635; www.ogrod.uj.edu.pl; ul Kopernika 27; adult/concession 9zł/5zł; ☉9am-7pm, greenhouses 10am-6pm Sat-Thu, museum 10am-2pm Thu & Fri, 11am-3pm Sun; 🚃4, 10, 14, 20, 44, 52)

History Land MUSEUM

5 ⦿ MAP P128, B3

Modern, kid-oriented historical exhibition that uses both LEGO building blocks and virtual-reality technology to tell key stories of Poland's national history in a way that engages the senses. The exhibition is located in the former main train station building. (☑530 903 053; www.historyland.pl; Plac Jana Nowaka Jeziorańskiego 3; adult/concession 27/24zł; ☉9am-5pm Mon-Fri, 10am-6pm Sat & Sun; 🚶; 🚃2, 3, 4, 5, 10, 14, 17, 19, 20, 44, 50, 52)

WowKrakow! BUS

6 ⦿ MAP P128, C6

Popular 'Hop-On Hop-Off' bus tour that allows passengers to stop at their leisure at some 15 different areas of interest around town. Buses depart hourly from near the Galeria Kazimierz. See the website for an up-to-date timetable and route. The parent company, **Jordan Group** (✆12 422 60 91; www.jordan.pl; ul Pawia 8; ⊙8am-6pm Mon-Fri, 9am-2pm Sat; 🚊3, 5, 17, 19, 50), also sells international bus tickets and airport transfers. (Jordan Group; ✆601 502 129; www.wowkrakow.pl; ul Gęsia 8; per 24/48hr 60/90zł; ⊙8am-6pm Mon-Fri; 🚊3, 19, 24)

SeeKrakow

TOURS

7 ◉ MAP P128, A5

SeeKrakow is the largest tour operator in Kraków and offers a bewildering array of guided tours, including tours of Schindler's Factory and the Rynek Underground, as well as day trips to the Auschwitz-Birkenau Memorial and Museum and Wieliczka Salt Mine. Check the website for details. Buy tickets at the office, online or at InfoKraków or SeeKrakow TIP tourist offices. (✆12 429 4499; www.seekrakow.com; ul Wielopole 16/3; ⊙8am-8pm; 🚊1, 3, 24, 52)

Park Wodny

SWIMMING

8 ◉ MAP P128, D2

Your skin will be wrinkled and prunelike by the time you leave this fun-filled indoor aqua park, located 2.5km northeast of the Old Town. For hours of wet and wild fun, there are paddling pools, watersports, 800m of water slides, saltwater hot tubs, saunas and more. Prices are a little higher Saturday and Sunday. (✆12 616 3190; www.parkwodny.pl; ul Dobrego Pasterza 126, Prądnik Czerwony; adult/concession per hr 28/24zł; per day incl sauna 67/55zł; ⊙8am-10pm; 👶; 🚊129, 152)

Eating

Pizza Garden

PIZZA $

9 ✕ MAP P128, B3

Arguably the best pizza in Kraków: the chef learned his pizza-making skills in New York. As you enter you'll see the large brick oven where the magic happens. At busy times you may have to queue for a seat, but it's worth it. (✆12 422 7755; www.pizzagarden.pl; ul Rakowicka 1; pizza 24-30zł; ⊙noon-10pm,

---

The Perfect Polish Sausage

The **Unitarg Hala Targowa** is home to the city's most famous late-night **sausage stand** (Kiełbaski Pod Halą Targową; Map p128, B5; ul Grzegórzecka 3; sandwiches 16zł; ⊙8pm-3am Mon-Sat; 🚊1, 17, 19, 22), and after a night of carousing you can bet that more than a few locals will make their way here for a snack before bed. The grilling begins at 8pm nightly (except Sunday) and runs till 3am. Look for two guys huddled over an open fire (and often with a long queue).

from 1pm Sat & Sun; 🛜🖊; 🚌2, 4, 10, 14, 20, 44, 52)

Novum Bistro
POLISH $$

10 ✕ MAP P128, C3

One of the better restaurants in this part of town, Novum Bistro goes for traditional but hard-to-find mains like rabbit, venison and wild boar, as well as the expected steaks, pastas and burgers. The owners pride themselves on their demanding wine and cocktail lists.They also have good breakfasts and decent-value multi-course lunch specials. (📞609 205 732; www.facebook.com/novumbistro; ul Lubicz 42; mains 30-50zł; ⏲8.30am-9pm; 🛜; 🚌4, 10, 14, 20, 44, 52)

Drinking

Zaraz Wracam Tu
COCKTAIL BAR

11 🚇 MAP P128, B6

Unfussy cocktail bar best known for the quality and variety of its shot drinks. The interior is big enough for groups, and there are occasional disco and live-music nights. (📞12 628 7510; www.zarazwracam.com; ul Miodowa 51a; ⏲3pm-2am; 🛜; 🚇3, 19, 24)

Wesoła Cafe
CAFE

12 🚇 MAP P128, B3

A real find, whether you happen to be staying out this way or just passing through. Excellent coffees as well as a full breakfast and lunch menu chock-full of healthy vegetarian and gluten-free options. The

Galeria Krakowska

atmosphere is busy but congenial, as mainly neighbourhood people dart in and out for a cup or a bite on their breaks. (513 932 810; www.wesolacafe.pl; ul Rakowicka 17; 7am-9pm, 8am-7pm Sat & Sun; ; 2)

Cat Café Kociarnia   CAFE

13 MAP P128, A3

Cosy place with coffee, tea, shakes and cakes – and several cats – all within a stone's throw of Kraków's Main Station. (795 010 130; www.lubicz.kociakawiarniakrakow.pl; ul Lubicz 1; 10am-8pm, 11am-9pm Sat & Sun; ; 2, 3, 4, 5, 10, 14, 17, 19, 20, 44, 50, 52)

Entertainment

Opera Krakowska   OPERA

14 MAP P128, C3

The Kraków Opera performs in the strikingly modern building at the Mogilski roundabout. The setting is decidedly 21st century, but the repertoire spans the ages, incorporating everything from Verdi to Bernstein. (12 296 6262; www.opera.krakow.pl; ul Lubicz 48; tickets 28-200zł; box office 10am-7pm Mon-Sat; 4, 5, 9, 10, 44, 52)

Shopping

Galeria Krakowska   SHOPPING CENTRE

15 MAP P128, A3

In case there was any question about Poland transitioning to capitalism, here's your answer. This massive mall near the train station

A Quiet Place By Night

After dark, most of Eastern Kraków rolls up the sidewalks. There are few destination clubs or restaurants in the area, and you'll likely only venture out here to eat if you happen to be staying at a neighbourhood hotel. The part of the district near Kazimierz is the most fruitful for decent pubs and bars. The exception to this might be for opera lovers, who'll certainly want to catch a performance at the Opera Krakowska in a strikingly modern setting in the far east of the district.

contains 270 stores; of interest to world-weary travellers are the food court and bookstore. (12 428 9902; www.galeriakrakowska.pl; ul Pawia 5; 9am-10pm, 10am-9pm Sun; ; 2, 3, 4, 10, 14, 20, 44, 52)

Krakowski Kredens   FOOD & DRINKS

16 MAP P128, A3

Within the Galeria Krakowska (p133) shopping centre and not far from the train station, take a look inside the 'Kraków cupboard' to find jars of traditional soups, as well as loads of edible souvenirs, such as marinated mushrooms, herb honey, spicy mustard and gooseberry preserves, to take with you on the train ride home. (696 490 017; www.krakowskikredens.pl; ul Pawia 5; 10.30am-5pm Mon-Sat; 2, 3, 4, 10, 14, 20, 44, 52)

Walking Tour

Workers' Paradise in Nowa Huta

A special gift from 'Uncle Joe' Stalin, the suburb of Nowa Huta ('New Steelworks') consisted of a massive steel mill and a socialist-realist residential area. It's a perfectly preserved example of utopian, communist-era housing. Far greener than it was in its heyday (1950s to 1970s), it's worth exploring to admire the grandiose scale and harmonious retro-futuristic architecture.

Walk Facts

Start Plac Centralny tram stop

End Klasztorna tram stop

Length 5km; four hours

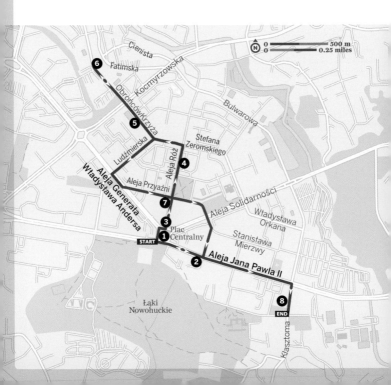

❶ 'Ronald Reagan Square'

Leave the tram at the quarter's main square, **Plac Centralny** (Plac Centralny im. Ronalda Reagana; Plac Centralny; 🚊 4, 10, 22, 44). This grandiose square, built in 1949, was once named for Stalin and dotted by a statue of Lenin. It's named after former US President (and Cold War warrior) Ronald Reagan.

❷ Muzeum PRL-u

Take a peek inside the **Muzeum of the People's Republic of Poland** (Muzeum PRL; 📞 12 446 7821; www. mprl.pl; Osiedle Centrum E1; adult/concession 10/8zł, free Tue; ⏰ 9am-4pm Mon-Fri), located in the 1950s socialist-realist Światowid cinema. There's a nuclear bunker in the basement.

❸ Alley of the Roses

The area's central avenue, **Aleja Róż** (Alley of the Roses), is a wide, parklike thoroughfare, where you can see the planners' intentions to glorify the workers.

❹ Nowa Huta Museum

North of Plac Centralny, the **Nowa Huta Museum** (📞 12 425 9775; www.mhk.pl; Osiedle Słoneczne 16; adult/concession 6/4zł, free Wed; ⏰ 9.30am-5pm Tue-Sun) features displays of Nowa Huta's past. They've plotted out area walking tours, where you can explore the individual housing estates.

❺ Theatre for the People

The 1950s and '60s were a period of architectural and theatrical experimentation. The **Teatr Ludowy** (People's Theatre; 📞 12 680 2101; www.ludowy.pl; Osiedle Teatralne 34; 🚊 1, 5) achieved both, with a startling socialist-realist exterior and daring repertoire.

❻ Church for the Workers

The brutalist **Arka Pana** (Lord's Ark; 📞 12 644 0624; www.arkapana.pl; ul Obrońców Krzyża 1; admission free; ⏰ 9am-6pm; 🚊 1, 5) was the first church in Nowa Huta. It was built in 1977 after a campaign by the local bishop (Karol Wojtyła, who would become Pope John Paul II).

❼ Dining in 'Style'

Nowa Huta is short on dining options, but **Restauracja Stylowa** (📞 12 644 2619; www.stylowa-krakow.pl; Osiedle Centrum C3; mains 24-30zł; 🚊 4, 10, 22, 44) offers the prospect of a worker's lunch amid the charmingly dated interior of the area's most elegant restaurant.

❽ Before the Mills

Walk east to ul Klasztorna, where an ancient ecclesiastical site beckons. The **Cistercian Abbey** (Opactwo Cystersów; 📞 12 644 2331; www.mogila.cystersi.pl; ul Klasztorna 11; admission free; ⏰ 9am-5pm; 🚊 10, 16, 21, 44) dates back to the year 1222.

Worth a Trip 👀
Auschwitz-Birkenau Memorial & Museum

The German Nazi Concentration and Extermination Camp of Auschwitz-Birkenau is synonymous with genocide and the Holocaust. More than a million Jews, plus many Poles and Roma, were murdered here by German occupiers during WWII. Both sections – the main camp Auschwitz I and a much larger outlying camp at Birkenau (Auschwitz II) – have been preserved and are open for visitors.

📞 guides 33 844 8100

tour adult/concession 60/55zł

🕐 7.30am-7pm Jun-Aug, to 6pm Apr-May & Sep, to 5pm Mar & Oct, to 4pm Feb, to 3pm Jan & Nov, to 2pm Dec

Auschwitz Main Gate

Tours begin in the visitors centre of the **main camp** with the screening of a graphic 17-minute documentary film on the liberation of the camp by Soviet soldiers in 1945; the film is not recommended for children under 14. The tour then proceeds through the infamous gates bearing the slogan '*Arbeit Macht Frei*' ('Work Sets You Free') to the main mustering point for the prisoners, where they would be called for morning roll and for camp announcements. The sign (pictured) is a replica, the original having been stolen, recovered, and put on display in the museum.

Barracks Exhibitions

The bulk of the exhibits in the main camp are located in former barracks, with each building (a 'block') given a number and a specific theme, such as how the camp was created, the confiscation of personal property, daily life, and the resistance movement. Each block holds its own horrors, such as photos of those who were killed or the tiny bunks where dozens of prisoners were forced to sleep. Nothing, however, is more appalling than the massive sea of human hair (in Block 4) that was collected from victims (usually just before their murder) and then used as an industrial material. The display, a mere fraction of what was found by the liberating Soviets, takes up half a long room.

Block 11 – the 'Death Block'

Block 11 is known as the notorious 'Death Block'. While most of the mass killings took place in Birkenau, it was here in this small courtyard where thousands of victims were lined up and shot in front of the Wall of Death. The basement contains cells where prisoners were tortured, held in solitary confinement and starved to death. At one end of the grounds, you can enter a gas chamber and

★ Top Tips

o From April to October it's compulsory to join a tour for entries between 10am and 3pm.

o A free shuttle bus runs between the two sites every 10 minutes from April to October, and every 30 minutes from November to March. Otherwise, it's an easy (but featureless) 2km walk between the two sites.

o Most travel agencies in Kraków offer organised tours to Auschwitz-Birkenau from 130zł per person, including transport and a guide.

✗ Take a Break

There are few snack bars near the main parking area, and a canteen-style restaurant near the main entrance.

★ Getting There

Minibus Services (12zł, 1¾ hours) leave from Kraków Bus Station to Auschwitz-Birkenau.

Train Services (16zł, 1½ hours) run from Kraków Main Station to Oświęcim.

crematorium – the only one not destroyed by the fleeing Germans in a vain attempt to hide their crimes.

Birkenau Main Gate & Tower

From the main camp, **Birkenau** – the largest of the outlying camps – is 2km to the west. Most of the mass killings actually took place at this vast expanse, which was purpose-built by the Germans as an extermination camp (at Auschwitz I, some prisoners were kept alive for as long as they could work as slaves). Although much of the camp was destroyed by the retreating Nazis near the end of WWII, the barracks that remained standing, the long perimeter of barbed wire and the endless rows of isolated chimneys convey the unthinkable scale of the killing. The main building at the entrance holds a small exhibition, and you can climb the tower for a view over the camp.

Birkenau Barracks

The real experience of Birkenau is simply walking through the camp, passing through the various sections, including separate parts for men, for women, and – perversely – a small section for 'families'. You can still see the train tracks that ran through the centre of the grounds, aligned for maximum efficiency of delivery and dispatch. It was here that the selection process took place: some passengers were sent to labour as slaves and live in the squalor of the barracks; others (in particular the

Baggage of Holocaust victims

A Short History Of the Holocaust

It's impossible to adequately encompass in words the slaughter of Europe's Jewish population by Nazi Germany, but some background is essential to understanding what Auschwitz-Birkenau actually is.

Early Stages

In the early stages of WWII, in 1940 and 1941, the Germans used camps such as Auschwitz to house political prisoners, including Poles. Polish Jews were restricted to purpose-built ghettos constructed in Warsaw, Łódź, Podgórze (Kraków) and scores of other cities. Living conditions in the ghettos were deliberately appalling, and thousands died.

From Internment to Extermination

After Germany declared war on the Soviet Union in 1941, Nazi policy toward the Jews shifted from internment to extermination. Here at Auschwitz, the Birkenau camp was built to function exclusively as a holding and extermination camp. By the end of 1942 and into early 1943, the majority of Poland's Jewry had been killed. The killings at Auschwitz-Birkenau and other places would grind on through 1944, but by then most of the victims were Jews from other European countries, including Hungary and France.

Supplementary Reading

Should your visit compel you to learn more about the Holocaust, there are many, many scholarly and personal writings that can help. For many, the gold standard remains Primo Levi's *If This is a Man*. Levi, an Italian Jew, survived the war as a prisoner in the Monowitz camp at Auschwitz and went on to become a writer of great renown.

To see the camps from a Polish perspective, pick up Tadeusz Borowski's *This Way for the Gas, Ladies and Gentlemen*. Borowski was not a Jew, but a Polish political prisoner.

old, the ill and young children) were immediately separated and sent directly to the gas chambers.

Central Baths & Gas Chambers

To the back of the Birkenau camp, you can visit the central camp baths and retrace the route of prisoners as they moved from the selection process to the gas chambers. Nearby are the ruins of the gas chambers, crematoria, and other places where corpses were burned in the open air and the ashes deposited in small ponds.

Worth a Trip 👀
Wieliczka Salt Mine

The Wieliczka Salt Mine is an eerie underground world of pits and chambers filled with finely crafted sculptures and bas-reliefs carved by hand from salt. It's been a Unesco World Heritage Site since 1978. First-time visitors go with a standard 'tourist' route of the highlights, while repeat visitors might opt for the more immersive 'miners' route. Both cost the same.

📞 12 278 7302

www.kopalnia.pl

ul Daniłowicza 10, Wieliczka

adult/concession 94/74zł

🕐 7.30am-7.30pm Apr-Oct, 8am-5pm Nov-Mar

Chapel of St Kinga

The 'tourist' route most visitors choose starts with a giddying descent down 380 wooden stairs to reach a depth of 135m. The showpiece is the ornamented Chapel of St Kinga (Kaplica Św Kingi), a church measuring 54m by 18m, and 12m high. Every element here, from chandeliers to altarpieces, is made of salt. It took more than 30 years to finish.

Erazm Barącz Chamber

This chamber, situated at a depth of 100m, has been partly flooded by a lake. The lake is some 9m deep and the water gives off an eerie green glow because of the saline content.

Stanisław Staszic Chamber

This enormous chamber measures 36m in height, and visitors can enjoy the scale from a lookout platform. The chamber has hosted extreme sporting events and even an underground balloon flight.

Kraków Saltworks Museum

The tour ends at the Kraków Saltworks Museum, accommodated in 14 chambers on level three, but most visitors seem to be over-salted by then. From here a mining lift takes you back up to the real world.

The 'Miners' Route

If you've been to the mine before, consider the more-immersive 'miners' route, where you explore less-visited parts of the mine while wearing standard mining gear. Groups of 20 visitors head off from the 'Regis Shaft' near the centre of Wieliczka. The tour takes three hours.

★ **Top Tips**

o The main tour takes two hours and covers about 3km.

o Bring a coat or sweater. The temperature in the mine is a chilly 15°C.

o English-language tours depart every 30 minutes from 8.30am to 6pm in summer, and less frequently the rest of the year.

o Buy tickets in advance online or turn to an InfoKraków office or your hotel for help.

o Several tour operators, including Cracow City Tours, run bus tours to the mine starting at around 150zł per person.

✕ **Take a Break**

Traditional Polish food is available underground at the **Miners' Tavern** in the Budryk Chamber.

★ **Getting There**

Bus 30 minutes from the main bus station.

Train 25 minutes from the main train station.

Survival Guide

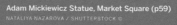

Adam Mickiewicz Statue, Market Square (p59)
NATALIYA NAZAROVA / SHUTTERSTOCK ©

Before You Go

Book Your Stay

○ Air-conditioning isn't necessary most of the year; the exception is July and August, when Kraków is prone to an occasional heat wave.

○ Parking anywhere near the centre can be tight. If driving, work out parking details with the hotel in advance.

○ To save money, consider booking a private single or double in a hostel.

○ If noise is an issue, ask for a room away from the street. Bear in mind that top-floor rooms, immediately below the roof, can get hot in summer.

○ Note that the more expensive hotels will sometimes quote prices in euros for convenience, but the bill is alway paid for in local currency, złoty.

Useful Websites

Most Kraków hotels and hostels list

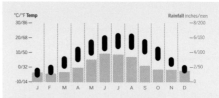

When to Go

○ **Winter** (Nov–Mar) Short, dark days, snow and blustery winds. Tourists descend for lively Christmas and New Year festivities.

○ **Spring** (Apr–Jun) April marks the start of the tourist season. Accommodation tightens over Easter.

○ **Summer** (Jul–Aug) Sunny and occasionally hot. Tourist levels in the Old Town swell to bursting.

○ **Autumn** (Sep–Oct) Occasionally sunny but cool. Some attractions close for winter.

through large global booking sites such as **Booking.com** (www.booking.com).

Noce.pl (www.noce.pl) National booking site is strong on apartment accommodation in Kraków.

InfoKraków (www.infokrakow.pl) Tourist office branches can help find rooms in a pinch.

Airbnb (www.airbnb.com) Global peer-to-peer apartment- and room-sharing service is very active in Kraków and has loads of listings.

Lonely Planet (lonelyplanet.com/poland/hotels) Recommendations and bookings.

Best Budget

Hostel Atlantis (www.atlantishostel.pl) Clean, good-value and excellent Kazimierz location.

Mundo Hostel (www.mundohostel.eu) Run by people who understand travel and what makes hostels special.

Pink Panther's Hostel (www.pinkpanthershostel.com) Pub crawls and party nights in the Old Town.

Ars Hostel (www. arshostel.pl) Can't beat the Wawel/Kazimierz location.

Goodbye Lenin Revolution Hostel (www.goodbyelenin.pl) Tongue-in-cheek kitsch and affordable private rooms.

Best Midrange

U Pana Cogito (www. pcogito.pl) Lovely setting in a manicured old manor.

Hotel Eden (www.hotel eden.pl) Best of several private hotels in the middle of Kazimierz.

Plaza Boutique Hotel (www.plazahotelkra kow.pl) Excellent value for money in the heart of Podgórze.

Hotel Pod Wawelem (www.hotelpod wawelem.pl) Some rooms look out onto Wawel Castle.

Grand Ascot Hotel (www.grandascot.pl) Gleaming outside and in; close to Western Kraków's clubs and the Old Town.

Best Top End

Metropolitan Boutique Hotel (www. hotelmetropolitan.pl) Mixes modern design within the luxury confines of a 19th-century townhouse.

Hotel Stary (www. stary.hotel.com.pl) Exudes charm, with lush period details like exposed-beam ceilings and shiny parquet flooring.

Hotel Copernicus (https://copernicus. hotel.com.pl) Swish Wawel offering, with fetching views from the rooftop terrace.

Hotel Pod Różą (www. podroza.hotel.com.pl) Exquisitely 'old world', with antiques and oriental carpets.

Arriving in Kraków

John Paul II International Airport

Sleekly modern **John Paul II International Airport** (KRK; ☑ 12 295 5800, 801 055 000; www. krakowairport.pl; ul Kapitana Mieczysława Medweckiego 1. Balice; 🛜) is located in Balice, about 15km west of the centre. The airport handles all domestic and international flights and has car-hire desks, bank ATMs, a tourist information office and currency exchanges.

Trains connect the airport with Kraków's Main Station (9zł, 20 minutes, every 30 minutes). They run daily from about 4am to midnight.

Bus 208 runs from the airport to Kraków's Main Bus Station (4.60zł, 45 minutes, hourly) between 4.30am and 10.30pm.

A **taxi** into the city centre should cost from 70zł to 90zł and take about 30 minutes.

Kraków Main Train Station

The modern **Kraków Main Station** (Kraków Główny; ☑ 22 391 9757; www.pkp.pl; ul Pawia 5a; 🛜; 🚊 2, 3, 4, 5, 10, 14, 17, 19, 20, 44, 50, 52) is on the northeastern edge of the Old Town, entered via the **Galeria Krakowska** (☑ 12 428 9902; www.galeriakrakowska.pl; ul Pawia 5; ⊙ 9am-10pm, 10am-9pm Sun; 🛜; 🚊 2, 3, 4, 10, 14, 20, 44, 52) shopping centre. Mostly underground, the station is beautifully laid out, with information booths and ticket offices on several levels. Find the left-luggage office (per day 6zł) and storage lockers (big/small locker per day 12/8zł) below platform 5. There are plenty of bank ATMs, restaurants and shops.

Walk The Old Town in about 10 minutes away by following ul Pawia south.

Trams Connecting the station to all parts of the city, most trams stop south of the station, on the northern edge of the Old Town, or along ul Pawia.

Kraków Bus Station

Kraków's **bus station** (📞703 403 340; www.mda.malopolska.pl; ul Bosacka 18; 📶; 🚊2, 3, 4, 5, 10, 14, 17, 19, 20, 44, 50, 52) is next to the main train station northeast of the Old Town. Access the station through the train station and follow the signs. The station has ticket and information counters, storage lockers and vending machines. Nearly all intercity coaches, both domestic and international, arrive at and depart from this station.

Walk to the Old Town in about 10 minutes by following ul Pawia south.

Trams connect the station to all parts of the city. Most trams stop south of the station, on the northern edge of the Old Town, or along ul Pawia.

Getting Around

Trams & Buses

○ The extensive transport network is operated by the **Kraków Public Transport Authority** (Miejskie Przedsiębiorstwo Komunikacyjne/MPK; 📞12 19150; www.mpk.krakow.pl).

○ The system runs daily from about 5am to 11pm.

○ Rides require a valid ticket that can be bought from automated ticketing machines (*automat biletów*) onboard or at some news agents and kiosks.

○ InfoKraków tourist offices can supply a transport map, though system maintenance and temporary re-routings are common and the map may be out of date.

Tickets & Passes

○ Tickets for trams and buses can be used interchangeably on both methods of transport.

○ Tickets for both are valid for various time periods, from 20 minutes (3.40zł) and 50 minutes (4.60zł) up to 24/48/72 hours (15/28/42zł).

○ Buy tickets from machines (*automat biletów*) onboard vehicles or at major transport stops. Some machines take only coins, while others allow you to pay with banknotes and credit cards too.

○ Validate your ticket in stamping machines when you first board the vehicle; spot checks are frequent and the fine for riding without a valid ticket is high (240zł).

Taxis

o Taxis are relatively inexpensive and a viable option for getting around.

o It's best to order a taxi by phone rather than hail one in the street. Only use marked cabs and always ask for a receipt at the end of the ride.

o In an honest cab, the meter starts at 7zł and rises by 2.30zł per kilometre, increasing to 3.50zł per kilometre from 10pm to 6am and on Sundays.

o App-based ride-share services like **Uber** and **Bolt** (Taxify) operate and can be slightly cheaper than licensed taxis.

o Reliable taxi companies that can handle phone requests in English include: **iTaxi** (℡73 773 7737; www.itaxi.pl) and **Radio Taxi Barbakan** (℡609 400 400; www.barbakan.krakow.pl).

Bicycle

o Kraków is relatively easy to negotiate by bike, though cars and trams are an ever-present danger.

o Marked cycling paths follow both sides of the river and circumnavigate the Old Town along the Planty.

o Several tourist agencies around town offer cycling tours. Info-Kraków tourist offices have free cycling maps.

o For rentals and tours, recommended outfitters include: **Dwa Koła** (℡12 421 5785; www.dwakola.internetdsl.pl; ul Józefa 5; per hr/day 7/50zł; ⏰10am-6pm; 🚃6, 8, 10, 13) and **Krk Bike Rental** (℡509 267 733; www.krkbikerental.pl; ul Św Anny 4; per hr/day 12/60zł; 🚃1, 6, 8, 13, 18).

o The city-wide bike-share programme, **Wavelo Kraków City Bike** (℡12 290 3333; www.en.wavelo.pl), offers payment schemes by the minute or for up to 12 hours. Find Wavelo bike stands all around town.

🔌 Essential Information

Accessible Travel

o Kraków has made remarkable progress in the past decade in improving access for travellers with disabilities.

o Most new buildings, including modern museums, galleries, shopping malls and train stations, are accessible and an increasing number of older buildings are being retrofitted.

o Kraków's Main Market Square and surrounding streets are now broadly accessible, with lots of smooth paving and kerb ramps.

o The Wieliczka Salt Mine has been modernised and is now wheelchair accessible.

o That said, high kerbs and stairs (especially at Wawel Castle) can still pose problems. Newer trams and buses are accessible, though some older trams are not. Many older buildings, including hotels and museums, are still not wheelchair friendly.

o Download Lonely Planet's free Accessible Travel guides from http://lptravel.to/AccessibleTravel.

Business Hours

Most places adhere to the following hours. Shopping centres generally have longer hours and are open from 9am to 8pm at weekends. Museums are often closed on Mondays and may have shorter hours outside of high season.

Banks 9am–4pm Monday to Friday, to 1pm Saturday

Offices 9am–5pm Monday to Friday, to 1pm Saturday

Post Offices 8am–7pm Monday to Friday, to 1pm Saturday

Restaurants 11am–10pm

Shops 8am–6pm Monday to Friday, 10am–2pm Saturday

Discount Cards

KrakowCard (www.krakowcard.com) Available online or from tourist information centres and costs 120/140zł for two/three days. Provides free transport on buses and trams and free entry to around 40 attractions, including Schindler's Factory, Rynek Underground, National Museum, St Mary's Church and the Eagle Pharmacy – but not Wawel Castle.

Electricity

Type E
220V/50Hz

Type C
220V/50Hz

Emergencies

Poland's country code	☏48
General emergency	☏112

Ambulance	☏999
Police	☏997
Fire	☏998

LGBT+ Travellers

Public attitudes in Poland toward LGBT+ individuals remain generally negative, and while homosexuality is legal in Poland, both the Catholic Church and ruling conservative government have opposed initiatives that would make it more acceptable to the public.

○ LGBT+ visitors are advised to exercise discretion and avoid public displays of affection.

○ Kraków has a small, but active LGBT+ population, with a handful of welcoming bars and clubs that change relatively frequently.

Money

The official Polish currency is the złoty, abbreviated to zł. It's divided into 100 groszy, abbreviated to gr. Banknotes come in denominations of 10zł, 20zł, 50zł, 100zł and 200zł, and coins in 1gr, 2gr, 5gr, 10gr,

Money-Saving Tips

o Plan the main meal of the day around lunch. Many restaurants offer specially discounted two- and three-course lunch menus.

o Take advantage of student-oriented vegetarian restaurants and traditional Polish milk bars (*bar mleczny*), where filling meals can be had for around 20zł.

o Many museums set aside one day a week for free admission.

o If you're planning on using trams extensively, purchase the heavily discounted 24-, 48- and 72-hour passes instead of using individual tickets.

20gr and 50gr, and 1zł, 2zł and 5zł. Hold on to coins and small notes for tram tickets and cafes.

ATMs

o ATMs are ubiquitous, particularly along main streets and in neighbourhood centres.

o ATMs accept most international cash cards. All ATMs require a four-digit PIN.

o Instead of exchanging bank notes, it can be cheaper simply to withdraw cash as needed from an ATM. Conversion fees are normally better than at banks or exchange counters.

Cash

o Change money at banks or *kantors* (private currency-exchange offices).

o Find these along main streets as well as at travel agencies, train stations and post offices. Rates vary, so it's best to shop around.

o *Kantors* are usually open between 9am and 6pm on weekdays and to 2pm on Saturday, but some open longer and a few stay open 24 hours.

Credit Cards

o Major credit cards, like Visa and MasterCard, are widely accepted. You may experience a problem with small transactions (under 10zł).

o American Express cards are typically accepted at larger hotels and restaurants, though they are not as widely recognised as other cards.

Tipping

o In restaurants, the norm is to tip 10% to reward good service. Leave the tip in the pouch the bill is delivered in or hand the money directly to the server.

o Tip hairdressers, tour guides and other personal services 10% of the total.

o Taxis drivers won't usually expect a tip, but it's fine to round the fare up to the nearest 5zł or 10zł increment for particularly good drivers.

Exchange Rates

Australia	A$1	2.71zł
Canada	C$1	2.84zł
Europe	€1	4.29zł
Japan	¥100	3.44zł
New Zealand	NZ$1	2.63zł
United Kingdom	£1	5.04zł
United States	US$1	3.80zł

For current exchange rates, see www.xe.com.

Dos & Don'ts

Fashion For sightseeing in Kraków, casual, comfortable clothing is the norm. Dress up for the opera or an evening out at a nice restaurant (a jacket for men, a skirt or pants suit for women). Smarten up for clubs to get by the bouncer at the door.

Religion Treat churches and monasteries with respect and stay silent inside. Wear proper attire, including trousers for men and covered shoulders and longer skirts (no short shorts) for women. Refrain from flash photography and be sure to leave a small donation at the door.

Public Transport Don't block the door on crowded trams. Always yield your seat to an elderly or disabled person or expectant mother.

Greetings It's customary to greet people on arriving with a friendly *dzień dobry!* (jyen do·bri; good day!) On leaving, part with a hearty *do widzenia!* (do vee·dze·nya; goodbye!).

Eating & Drinking When raising a glass, greet your friends with *na zdrowie!* (nah zdroh·vee·ya; cheers)! Before tucking into your food, wish everyone *smacznego!* (smach·neh·go; bon appetit)! End the meal with *dziękuję* (jyen·koo·ye; thank you).

Public Holidays

New Year's Day 1 January

Epiphany 6 January

Easter Sunday March or April

Easter Monday March or April

State Holiday 1 May

Constitution Day 3 May

Pentecost Sunday Seventh Sunday after Easter

Corpus Christi Ninth Thursday after Easter

Assumption Day 15 August

All Saints' Day 1 November

Independence Day 11 November

Christmas 25 and 26 December

Safe Travel

Kraków is generally a safe city for travellers, although as a major tourist spot it has its fair share of pickpockets; be vigilant in crowded public areas.

○ In summer, large numbers of tourists can mean long queues for top sights, such as Schindler's Factory and Wawel Royal Castle.

○ Some sights allow you to book your admission in advance over the web or assign you a slotted arrival time. These can greatly reduce wait times.

Telephone Services

Domestic & International Calls

○ Poland's country code is 📞48.

○ All telephone numbers, landline and mobile, have nine digits. It's not necessary to dial a 📞0 before calling between cities within Poland. Simply dial the unique nine-digit number.

o To call abroad from Poland, dial the international access code ☎00, then the country code, then the area code and number. To dial Poland from abroad, dial your country's international access code, then 48 and then the nine-digit local number.

Mobile Phones

o Poland uses the GSM 900/1800 system, the same as Europe, Australia and New Zealand. It's not compatible with some phones from North America or Japan; check with your service provider.

o Instead of paying your home provider's expensive roaming fees for data and calls, a cheaper option can be to purchase and install a local prepaid SIM card. They sell for as little as 10zł and can be set up quickly and painlessly.

o Before purchasing a SIM card, be sure your phone is unlocked (able to accept foreign SIM cards).

Toilets

o Public toilets are labelled 'toaleta' or 'WC', and are generally clean and well-kept.

o Men should look for 'dla panów' or 'męski', or a door marked by downward-pointing triangle.

o Women should head for 'dla pań' or 'damski', or a door marked with a circle.

o Public toilets often charge a fee of 2zł, collected by a toilet attendant sitting at the door. Have small change ready.

Tourist Information

o **InfoKraków** (www. infokrakow.pl), the official tourist information office, has branches all around town.

o Expect cheerful service, free maps and help in sorting out accommodation and transport. Some branches offer free wi-fi.

o Find branches at many convenient tourist locations, including at the **Cloth Hall** (☐12 354 2716; www.infokrakow. pl; Cloth Hall, Rynek Główny 1/3; ⏰9am-7pm May-Oct,

to 5pm Nov-Apr; 📶; 🚌1, 6, 8, 13, 18), **Kazimierz** (☐12 354 2728; www. infokrakow.pl; ul Józefa 7; ⏰9am-5pm; 📶; 🚌6, 8, 10, 13), **Nowa Huta** (☐12 354 2714; www.infokrakow. pl; Osiedle Zgody 7, Nowa Huta; ⏰10am-7pm; 📶; 🚌4, 10, 22, 44), **Old Town** (☐12 354 2725; www. infokrakow.pl; ul Św Jana 2; ⏰9am-7pm; 📶; 🚌1, 6, 8, 13, 18) and the **Airport** (☐12 285 5341; www. infokrakow.pl; John Paul II International Airport, Balice; ⏰9am-7pm; 📶).

Visas

o Citizens of EU countries do not need visas to visit Poland and can stay indefinitely.

o Citizens of the USA, Canada, Australia, New Zealand and many other countries can stay in Poland for up to 90 days without a visa.

o Other nationalities should check current visa requirements with the Polish embassy or consulate in their home country.

o There's more information on the Polish **Ministry of Foreign Affairs** (www.gov.pl/web/ diplomacy) website.

Language

Poland is linguistically one of the most homogeneous countries in Europe – more than 95% of the population has Polish as their first language. Polish belongs to the Slavic language family, with Czech and Slovak as close relatives. It has about 45 million speakers.

Vowels are generally pronounced short, giving them a 'clipped' quality. Note that **a** is pronounced as the 'u' in 'cut', **ai** as in 'aisle' and **ow** as in 'cow'. If you read the pronunciation guides in this chapter as if they were English you'll be understood just fine. Note that stressed syllables are indicated with italics.

To enhance your trip with a phrasebook, visit **lonelyplanet.com**.

Basics

Hello.
Cześć.   cheshch

Goodbye.
Do widzenia.   do vee·*dze*·nya

Yes./No.
Tak./Nie.   tak/nye

Please./You're welcome.
Proszę.   *pro*·she

Thank you.
Dziękuję.   jyen·*koo*·ye

Excuse me./Sorry.
Przepraszam.   pshe·*pra*·sham

How are you?
Jak pan/pani   yak pan/*pa*·nee
się miewa? (m/f)   shye *mye*·va

Fine. And you?
Dobrze.   *dob*·zhe
A pan/pani? (m/f)   a pan/*pa*·nee

Do you speak English?
Czy pan/pani   chi pan/*pa*·nee
mówi po   *moo*·vee po
angielsku? (m/f)   po an·*gyel*·skoo

I don't understand.
Nie rozumiem.   nye ro·*zoo*·myem

Eating & Drinking

I'd like the menu, please.
Proszę o   *pro*·she o
jadłospis.   ya·*dwo*·spees

I don't eat meat
Nie jadam   nye *ya*·dam
mięsa   *myen*·sa

Cheers!
Na zdrowie!   na *zdro*·vye

Please bring the bill.
Proszę o   *pro*·she o
rachunek.   ra·*khoo*·nek

Shopping

I'd like to buy ...
Chcę kupić ...   khtse *koo*·peech

I'm just looking.
Tylko oglądam.   *til*·ko o·*glon*·dam

How much is it?
Ile to kosztuje?   *ee*·le to kosh·*too*·ye

That's too expensive.
To jest za drogie. to yest za dro·gye

Can you lower the price?
Czy może pan/ chi mo·zhe pan/
pani obniżyć pa·nee ob·nee·zhich
cenę? (m/f) tse·ne

Emergencies

Help!
Na pomoc! na po·mots

Go away!
Odejdź! o·deyj

Call the police!
Zadzwoń po zad·zvon' po
policję! po·lee·tsye

Call a doctor!
Zadzwoń po zad·zvon' po
lekarza! le·ka·zha

I'm lost.
Zgubiłem/ zgoo·bee·wem/
am się. (m/f) wam shye

I'm ill.
Jestem yes·tem
chory/a. (m/f) kho·ri/ra

Where are the toilets?
Gdzie są toalety? gjye som to·a·le·ti

Time & Numbers

What time is it?
Która jest ktoo·ra yest
godzina? go·jee·na

It's one o'clock.
Pierwsza. pyerf·sha

Half past (10).
Wpół do fpoow do
(jedenastej). (ye·de·nas·tey)

morning
rano ra·no

afternoon
popołudnie po·po·wood·nye

evening
wieczór vye·choor

yesterday
wczoraj fcho·rai

today
dziś/dzisiaj jeesh/jee·shai

tomorrow
jutro yoo·tro

1	*jeden*	ye·den
2	*dwa*	dva
3	*trzy*	tshi
4	*cztery*	chte·ri
5	*pięć*	pyench
6	*sześć*	sheshch
7	*siedem*	shye·dem
8	*osiem*	o·shyem
9	*dziewięć*	jye·vyench
10	*dziesięć*	jye·shench

Transport & Directions

Where's a/the ...?
Gdzie jest ...? gjye yest ...

What's the address?
Jaki jest adres? ya·kee yest ad·res

Can you show me (on the map)?
Czy może pan/ chi mo·zhe pan/
pani mi pa·nee mee
pokazać po·ka·zach
(na mapie)? (m/f) (na ma·pye)

When's the next (bus)?
Kiedy jest kye·di yest
następny nas·temp·ni
(autobus)? (ow·to·boos)

A ... ticket (to Katowice).
Proszę bilet pro·she bee·let
... (do Katowic). ... (do ka·to·veets)

Behind the Scenes

Send Us Your Feedback

We love to hear from travellers – your comments help make our books better. We read every word, and we guarantee that your feedback goes straight to the authors. Visit **lonelyplanet.com/contact** to submit your updates and suggestions.

Note: We may edit, reproduce and incorporate your comments in Lonely Planet products such as guidebooks, websites and digital products, so let us know if you don't want your comments reproduced or your name acknowledged. For a copy of our privacy policy visit lonelyplanet.com/privacy.

Mark's Thanks

I'd like to thank the staff at the InfoKraków tourist offices for their information and recommendations. Special thanks to my friend Olga Brzezińska and her friend, Anna Szybist, formerly of Kraków City Hall, for their tips and assistance. Thanks as well to my friends throughout Poland for their support, and to my co-writers on the Poland project. One last thanks to my Destination Editor Gemma Graham, who offered me the project in the first place.

Acknowledgements

Cover photograph: Old Town (p51), kilhan/Getty Images ©

Photographs pp30–31 (clockwise from top left): Marcin_Kadziolka / Getty Images; Jaroslav Moravcik / Shutterstock; LALS STOCK / Shutterstock ©

This Book

This 3rd edition of Lonely Planet's *Pocket Kraków* guidebook was researched and written by Mark Baker, who also wrote the previous edition. This guidebook was produced by the following:

Destination Editor
Gemma Graham

Senior Product Editors
Sandie Kestell,
Genna Patterson

Regional Senior Cartographer Valentina Kremenchutskaya

Product Editors Joel Cotterell, Shona Gray

Book Designer
Wibowo Rusli

Assisting Editors
Andrew Bain, Judith Bamber, Nigel Chin, Samantha Forge, Carly Hall, Gabrielle Innes, Kellie Langdon, Rosie Nicholson, Lauren O'Connell, Kristin Odijk, Tamara Sheward, Gabrielle Stefanos

Cover Researcher
Naomi Parker

Thanks to Imogen Bannister, Rob Button, Martin Jacobs, Allyson Lees, Charlotte Orr, Dawn Simpson, Tracey Stubbins

Index

See also separate subindexes for:

◈ **Eating p157**

◉ **Drinking p158**

✪ **Entertainment p158**

◐ **Shopping p159**

🏷Shopping

A

Antykwariat na Kazimierzu 99
Asortyment Shop 99
Austeria 99

B

Błażko Jewellery Design 83
Boruni 75
Boruni Gallery 49

D

Dydo Poster Gallery 125

G

Galeria Dyląg 74
Galeria Krakowska 133
Galeria Plakatu 74

K

Kacper Ryx 74
Kobalt Pottery & More 49
Krakowski Kredens 133

L

Lookarna Illustrations 99

M

Marka 83
Massolit Books & Cafe 125

P

Paon Nonchalant 98
Plac Nowy Flea Market 98

R

Rubin 75

S

Salon Antyków Pasja 75
Schubert World of Amber 49
Starmach Gallery 113
Stary Kleparz 125
Stary Sklep 99
Szpeje 83

V

Vanilla 83

Ou

Lonely Planet pocket
02/26/2020

a penchant
for off beat stories and forgotten places. He's originall
from the United States, but now makes his home in th
Czech capital, Prague. He writes mainly on Eastern an
Central Europe for Lonely Planet as well as other leading travel publishers, but finds real satisfaction in dig-
ging up stories in places that are too remote or quirky
for the guides. Prior to becoming an author, he worked
as a journalist for *The Economist*, *Bloomberg News* and
Radio Free Europe, among other organisations.
Instagram & Twitter: @markbakerprague
Blog: www.markbakerprague.com

Contributing Writer

Hugh McNaughtan wrote the Auschwitz-Birkenau
Memorial & Museum feature.

Published by Lonely Planet Global Limited
CRN 554153
3rd edition – Feb 2020
ISBN 978 1 78657 582 1
© Lonely Planet 2020   Photographs © as indicated 2020
10 9 8 7 6 5 4 3 2 1
Printed in Singapore